HOW TO ESTABLISH
AND DOCUMENT
THE BEST KNOWN
WAY TO DO A JOB

PROCESS MASTERING

RAY W. WILSON, P.E.
AND PAUL HARSIN

PRODUCTIVITY
productivity press

Printed in the United States of America

07 06 05 04 03   10 9 8 7 6 5 4

ISBN 0-527-76344-6

Library of Congress Cataloging-in-Publication Data

Wilson, Ray W.
        Process mastering : how to establish and document the best
known way to do a job / Ray W. Wilson, Paul Harsin.
                p.   cm.
        Includes index.
        ISBN 0-527-76344-6 (alk. paper)
        1. Total quality management.   2. Customer services.   3. Consumer
satisfaction.   4. Competition.   I. Harsin, Paul, 1946–   .   II. Title.
HD62.15.W554   1998
658.5'62—dc21
                                                            97-47365
                                                            CIP

We dedicate this book to our families—the present generation for their support and encouragement and the past generations for their nurturing and wisdom.

Ray W. Wilson
Paul Harsin

CONTENTS

PREFACE

"The business world is changing faster than ever before. We intend to help as many people as possible to cope, to improve the way business is done, and to work with customers in an unending cycle of continual improvement." Those words, or variations of them, have been said by dozens of authors for the past 15 years. We feel the need to restate them and provide an example, which is based on an experience of one of the authors.

A few months ago, I bought a lake cottage in northern Indiana, on the shore of Turkey Lake. The former owner had left a telephone, but the wire from the street to the house had been broken by an ice storm. When he called the telephone business office, the new owner told Millie, the customer representative, the situation, giving the name of the previous owner and requesting new service. I explained the wire was down and the line was dead, and gave the address as "136 Lakeside Drive, Turkey Lake, LaGrange . . ." Since the lake was somewhat remote, I gave explicit driving directions, even to the exact intersection of streets where the cottage stands. Millie put the driving directions in the "Remarks" section of the customer order and set a date for service to begin.

On the appointed date, the service truck never came. Late that afternoon, I called the telephone company about the appointment. Ralph, another customer representative, informed me that the computer showed the line would now be working at the cottage.

Back at the cottage, the line still dangled from the pole and was still not connected to the house. I returned to the pay phone and called the telephone company back, and this time I was routed to repair service. The repair representative, Mary, assured me that the phone was working. I informed her that it definitely was not working, because the line was still broken. Mary assured me that it would be fixed by noon the next morning.

The service truck arrived at 8:15 the next morning. The serviceman explained that the customer service representatives were in northern Ohio, and the service department's representative was in western Indiana. He was the only telephone company employee within 65 miles of LaGrange or Turkey Lake and apologized for the service delay. Apparently, he had installed the phone in a vacant house behind the hospital in LaGrange, because that is where the service order requested it. He continued, "I told Millie that there was something wrong with this address before I left the office. The address was on Parkview in LaGrange, but the driving directions sent me here. She said not to worry about it, she had checked it against the service records of the old owner. *The new owner lives in Indianapolis. He must be mistaken about where the cottage is located.*"

Jack, the serviceman, continued, "I went to the address behind the hospital, and the place looked like it was deserted, with trash and broken windows. I called in on the radio and told them this was the wrong place, that the driving directions and the address did not agree. Millie's supervisor told me the phone had to be installed at the address on the service order, no matter what the customer said in the 'Remarks' section." He had installed the telephone, and when Mary had checked the line had been working—at 136 Parkview Avenue, the deserted house with broken windows, behind the hospital.

Before leaving, Jack fixed the wire and checked the phone. From the telephone company's perspective, everything was all right.

This miscommunication between the customer and the telephone company is an example of the breakdown that often happens between suppliers and customers. Today's businesses face pulls and tugs that can break communications lines. Distances increase, making it more difficult.

We wrote this book to help overcome the forces that split organizations and their customers apart. In process mastering, there is a great deal of focus on the needs and desires of customers. There is an opportunity for customers to actually participate in developing process masters. We believe workers understand the details of their jobs, but time and distance can undermine their efforts. We intend to help organizations and workers refocus process expertise on meeting customer needs to help everyone succeed.

Is the rate of quality improvement satisfactory in your organization? If not, this is our effort to help you speed up the rate of change. By using everyone's energy, skills, thoughts, ambition, expertise, and cooperation, tomorrow's organizations will perform more smoothly, and customers will be more satisfied than ever before.

Ray W. Wilson
Paul Harsin
January 1998

ACKNOWLEDGMENTS

We thank Karen Hall for multiple retypes of our manuscript and for her constant encouragement. We thank Cindy Wilson for her ruthless editing and proofreading. She kept us focused on the subject. We thank the employees of Countrymark Cooperative, Inc., and Universal Flavors who helped us hone the ideas and theory of the book. We thank our fellow learners of the Indy Quality, Productivity and Involvement Council for generously sharing their knowledge and experiences with us.

We also thank those who read our manuscript and made numerous suggestions to improve it: Peter Scholtes, Dr. Tom Cooke, John Homer, Rick Kivett, Tim Baer, Bill Shakal, Ron Moen, Mike Jerrell, Dudley Keen, Lou Schultz, Dr. Harold Haller, Dave Church, Carolyn Bailey, Don Curtis, Dr. Brenda Frye, Deborah Hearn Smith, Glade Wilkes, and John McConnell.

Chapter 1

LAYING THE FOUNDATION: THE AIM OF THIS BOOK

Workers want to do good work, and they know best the details of doing their jobs. We are offering a method to utilize their knowledge in a way that helps everyone in the organization be successful.

We define process mastering as a discipline that focuses on reducing variation and increasing knowledge of processes through the efforts of experts, linking customers and suppliers. In this case, the experts are the people who do the work in the process every day. These people, in a short amount of time, can arrive at the best known way to do their work. In doing so, they will consider what internal and external customers want, what the process needs from its suppliers, and what is required of everyone who works in the process. The result of their brief effort is a process master that can be the foundation for continual improvement of the process.

Process mastering is a simple but powerful basic procedure available to anyone wanting to improve. We commend it to your attention.

Desired Outcome

With this tool, supervisors and workers will be able to communicate in an open, nonthreatening, and constructive manner. Activities that cross department or process boundaries will become clearer, cleaner, less contentious, and will result in fewer balls being dropped. Quality of output will be clearly seen by the customer. The organization will learn faster and more consistently. A culture valuing long-term, steady improvement will flourish. Fewer workers will be injured on the job. Workers will have more pride and joy in their work, and profits will improve.

This is a substantial vision for such a simple procedure. Be assured, the items in this vision are eminently achievable.

Many organizations are still not adapting fast enough to a customer-centered economy where customers can buy from any one of a dozen excellent suppliers. A few years ago, customers were thought of as a collective pain in the neck. Today, we recognize and understand that they represent the only way an organization can stay in business. Today, quality of product and service is the price of admission to the market. And today, you may have a stable customer base. Tomorrow, however, your customers may move to another supplier in search of higher quality, lower prices, reliable delivery, and more dependable service—without you even sensing you have a problem.

How can you retain such fickle, demanding customers? How can you out-compete the world-class giants? What weapons can you pull out of your sleeve to beat your competition?

Computer technology? Can you develop overwhelming market strength with the latest computer technology? Probably not. Anyone with capital can get good computer systems.

Miracle automation? It may help temporarily, but without optimizing the process, robots may be doing unnecessary tasks faster than workers did before. Companies that go the automation route foster an arms race with their competitors.

Low-cost labor? Factoring in transportation, productivity, and quality of output, labor costs are becoming more uniform around the world.

> "Without a standard, there is no logical basis for making a decision or taking action."
>
> Joseph Juran

New markets in the Orient? There are lots of potential customers in China, but they must somehow acquire disposable income if they are to buy your product.

Faster application of process knowledge? Now you're on the track. "The ability to learn faster than your competitors may be the only sustainable competitive advantage" (Arie de Geus). We believe that continuously improving processes is critical to future success.

∧ Focus on the Process

> "At the end of the day, a company is the processes through which it creates value."
>
> Michael Hammer

In 1982, IBM began to focus on process improvement as a way to enhance their competitiveness. Kane wrote about IBM's customer demands: "Customers had higher expectations, competitors were delivering increasingly better products, and it was prohibitively expensive to fix problems." They began a business focus on processes as a way to become more competitive. Kane and his group observed some fundamental characteristics about work processes involving people:

- Processes adapt over time toward comfort, rather than toward competitiveness.

- Everyone works within a process and someone must be responsible for every process.

- The elements of any process, that the manager controls—people, materials, information, and techniques—are applied with great variability.

Some symptoms indicating poor process health are:

- Internal and external customer complaints
- Returns and declining customer satisfaction
- Things that have to be done over again
- Problems that never get resolved
- Missed deadlines
- Worsening morale and staff turnover
- Exceeded budgets and declining productivity
- Unproductive contention between individuals and/or departments
- Adding manpower as a solution to problems
- Systems that can't handle the current workload
- Unsatisfactory audits.

> "Processes left unregulated will change, but that change will be for the convenience of the people in the process rather than in the best interest of the organization or the customer. Comfort and control, instead of effectiveness and prudent risk-taking, become the rule."
>
> H.J. Harrington

Getting Better Results

It has been our experience that when variation in any work process is reduced, the results get better. Variation is believed to result from people, methods, materials, machines, the environment, and their interactions. Process mastering reduces the variation caused by people and methods, making it much easier to find the causes of variation in the other three factors. If we can eliminate differences in methods, where methods are important, we can

> "If I had to reduce my message to just a few words, I'd say it all had to do with reducing variation."
>
> Dr. W. Edwards Deming

reduce the variation from this source. At the same time, process mastering helps people understand their work better. Developing a process master is not making a wish list of how you would like the process to be; rather, it is capturing the *best known way* and putting it into practice. Process mastering improves the quality of output.

Why Process Mastering Works

Think for a minute about organizations you know. Do they have any standard operating procedures (SOPs)? Many organizations, especially small entrepreneurial businesses, have never documented their procedures at all. Who writes most SOPs? The engineers and managers? Who reads them? Are they used by process workers? What happens to most SOPs? We have observed that many are put on a shelf or in a file cabinet for years. When a new manager arrives in the office, the old SOPs may be dusted off and read. By this time, they have no relationship to the actual working processes. The old SOPs are junked and the cycle starts anew.

Imagine a common situation for a moment. Six workers make widget frames. If each of those people have been working on the process for a couple of years, there are probably six different ways of making the frames. One flips the frame over after assembly and pounds it twice with a hammer to even it out. Two others squeeze their frame pieces together by tightly pushing in on two ends while clamping. The rest use a variety of methods based on what works best for them today. If the SOP has not been changed in those two years, it probably is outdated.

This lack of working standards leads to confusion, variation in quality and quantity of output, and unnecessary costs.

> "There are three basic reasons why a person fails in performing his or her job.
>
> 1. The worker does not know what the job is.
> 2. The worker does not know how to do the job.
> 3. Something or someone interferes with the worker's ability to do the job."
>
> Steven Brown

It can also mean longer training times, more customer complaints, higher turnover rates, lower morale, higher accident rates, production rates not meeting expectations, longer cycle times, more scrap, and less supervisory control. The longer the process continues without current standards, the less manageable the process becomes.

Process masters are written by the workers and supervisors, with the expectation that these documents will be the basis of the next set of process masters. The focus of process mastering is not on writing strict standards, but on guiding the workers to write living standards. Process masters are expected to be superseded and are written for easy updating. Process masters are usually posted near the work areas. Since workers own the process masters, they will follow them more diligently than the old SOPs.

Process mastering is not designed to regiment people into mindless compliance, and it is not standardization for the sole purpose of having rigid standards. In our experience, having rigid job descriptions or standards restricting areas of responsibility reduces cooperation and adaptation to changing demands.

Process mastering is definitely *not* to be thought of as primarily a way of eliminating workers' jobs. If it is used this way, it will be unsuccessful. Neither is it a way of transferring the responsibility for quality improvement away from leaders. As with any effective management philosophy, leaders need to be involved.

Process mastering also adds value in hidden ways. Many important factors are not easily measurable. Here are some examples, paraphrased from *Out of the Crisis* (pp. 121–122).

- The multiplying effect on sales that comes from having a happy customer.

- The boost in productivity that comes from successful improvement of quality upstream from the process.

- The improvement in quality and productivity that results from continual improvement in processes and from better training and supervision.

- The improvement in quality and lower costs resulting from a team including the supplier, the process experts, and the customer, working together to improve parts and products.

- The improvement in productivity resulting from a team including the supplier, engineering, research and development, workers, and the customer working to reduce unneeded process steps.

Fundamental Building Block for Continual Improvement

> "Without standards, improvement potential is very much limited. Things will fall back to a chaotic state and there may be only firefighting work left for us to do."
>
> Kiyoshi Suzaki

Managers have asked us, "Isn't it enough to have cross-functional process-improvement teams working on problem processes?" Actually, we have not found this to work very well. Our experience has shown that processes must be standardized before process improvements can take root. When our early cross-functional process improvement teams were convened to improve out-of-control processes, the teams floundered along for months and years. They were shooting at moving targets. The teams tampered with the processes and collected new data every week. The teams made short-term gains in costs or cycle time, but when the attention turned to other processes, the improvements evaporated. Changes were definitely made, but long-term fixes were scarce. Where changes were made, the processes drifted back to the old way of doing things almost overnight.

Starting in the 1980s, IBM, Panasonic, Union Carbide, and other companies learned to standardize the processes first, then to measure key process factors. By using the suggestions developed during a process mastering cycle, workers enthusiastically followed the standards until they wrote new ones incorporating the improvements. Process mastering focused attention on key measures of process performance. Workers collected key data about the health of the process for an ade-

> "There can be no improvement without standards. The starting point in any improvement is to know exactly where one stands. There must be a precise standard of measurement for every worker, every machine and every process. Similarly, there must be a precise standard of measurement for every manager. Even before introducing TQC [Total Quality Control] and the Kaizen strategy, management must make an effort to understand where the company stands and what the work standards are. This is why standardization is one of the most important pillars of TQC."
>
> Masaaki Imai

quate length of time. Finally, after collecting adequate data, the teams started a process-improvement cycle and achieved both short-term and long-term gains.

Identifying Problems for Attention

If you believe your organization has a unique set of problems, you are not alone. We have been exposed to the organizational problems of more than 100 companies through the meetings of the Indy Quality, Productivity and Involvement Council, a quality improvement user group in Indianapolis. Every organization we have worked with thought they had a unique situation. Much of the time, however, the problems have been similar from company to company. Many service and manufacturing process problems related to three general areas:

- Lack of understanding of customer needs and wishes

- Lack of process understanding at the management and worker level

- Lack of process control measurements in key areas.

Processes requiring attention fall into one or more of the following categories:

1. The process is a safety or environmental concern.

2. The organization's plan calls for improvement in a certain area or process.

3. The process causes dissatisfaction for internal or external customers.

4. The process is new and has never been done before.

5. The process is known to have changed.

6. The process needs to be standardized and documented for certification or regulatory reasons.

If the process does not fall into at least one of these categories, then the required time and energy should be applied to some other improvement effort.

Long-Term Growth of Organizational Effectiveness

> "Learning is less fearful than failure in battle. Learning has a higher value here; it's recognized as a source of safety."
>
> Margaret Wheatley

You can generate successes like these in your own organization. The examples in this book are practical, quantifiable improvements documented by our clients and organizations. The savings in time and capital, and the customer benefits, are obvious.

What is not so obvious is profoundly more important to the long-term survival of organizations using our process mastering methods. Successful companies developed employees who were not afraid to make suggestions or to change their ways. Those workers were accumulating process knowledge, becoming process experts, and process managers. Rather than following the same old ruts, they challenged the system and improved it for everyone.

The employees we have described in this book have learned to focus on the needs of their internal and external customers. They have learned to work together as teams. Where the Lone Ranger paradigm had been the only way to operate for decades, workers learned to work toward the common good. Where workers were once thought of as "a pair of hands," they are now valued for their thinking ability.

When the standards no longer reflected the best way to do a job, the workers rewrote the standards and then improved the process, in an unending cycle of standardization and improvement. This change in an organization's rules for success can mean the long-term survival of the organization. Your organization will benefit in many ways, such as improved worker morale and motivation, when your workers take responsibility for their own processes.

Building Organizational Knowledge

"Managers often suboptimize their most valuable asset when they forget to use employees' brains. If leaders say they want the whole person, but act like they want only the body, they undermine their own most precious asset—credibility."

Lou Schultz

A defunct company where one of the authors worked used to be a great training ground for quality control employees. New science graduates would be hired and trained for a year or two. Then, most of them would leave for greener pastures. Continuity of talent was difficult to maintain. As each scientist learned methods and skills, he or she became more effective, a more valuable employee. When the employee left, a knowledge void was created in the department, and the manager would scramble for a replacement.

That company was not alone in using a low-salary strategy to control costs. In 1971, this was a common way to staff a quality department.

The costs of such a strategy only became obvious when the company was bought out, closed, and all employees lost their jobs.

This discontinuous or eyelash learning curve is shown in Figure 1. The employees spend time learning about the process and then transfer out of the department or leave the company, taking their skills and knowledge with them. More employees are trained and the cycle repeats itself. The organization has no

Figure 1. Eyelash Learning Curve

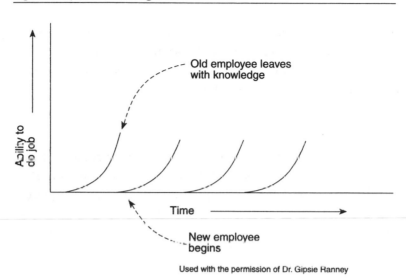

Used with the permission of Dr. Gipsie Ranney

process memory. No method exists for new learning to continue where the old employees left off. Every company has employees who know which button to press and valve to tweak to get production singing along. Those employees are more effective than any other workers; every worker has knowledge and skills that need to be enhanced and recorded, yet no method is used to preserve those years of experience.

Figure 2. Rapid Learning Curve

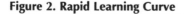

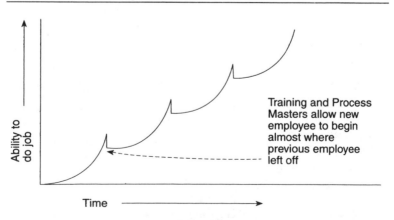

Used with the permission of Dr. Gipsie Ranney

A much more profitable curve is seen in Figure 2. This rapid learning curve allows organizations to advance by using living standards that are updated at every improvement. Organizations using the rapid learning curve have less turnover, less complexity, less waste, and more profits (Joiner). An organization can use process mastering to build its own rapid learning curve.

Summary

Customers will continue to demand more value in goods and services. Process mastering is a way to meet that demand more efficiently. It is a common-sense approach that requires little preparation and training. The process captures what the workers are already doing. They often don't have to struggle to find a solution to a problem. Because of this, momentum for change builds quickly. Workers buy into the continual improvement process because it affects their work directly. Process mastering helps to set up the organization for process improvement, suggestion systems, and preventive maintenance.

"Training and standardization create a nice positive spiral. A high degree of standardization is needed to make training possible. Without standardization, training is cumbersome, inefficient, and generally ineffective. And without effective training, any standard is soon lost."

Brian Joiner

The First Steps

To learn how you can use the process mastering steps, turn to Chapter 2. Management's role in process mastering (Chapter 3) gives guidelines for setting process-improvement priorities. Tricks and Traps (Chapter 4) gives useful advice for team sponsors and leaders, as well as for workers on teams. If you are interested in measuring organizational health or in examples of process mastering in use, see Chapter 5. The use of process mastering with ISO 9000 and other standard systems is discussed in Chapter 6. Each chapter is meant to stand alone, so feel free to start with whatever chapter interests you most.

References

Brown, W. S. (1987). *13 Fatal Errors Managers Make and How You Can Avoid Them*. New York: Berkeley.

de Geus, A. (1988). "Planning As Learning," *Harvard Business Review*, March/April, pp. 70–74.

Deming, W. E. (1986). *Out of the Crisis*. Cambridge, MA: MIT Center For Advanced Engineering Study, pp. 121–122.

Hammer, M. (1996). *Beyond Re-engineering*. New York: HarperBusiness, p. 197.

Harrington, H. J. (1991). *Business Process Improvement: The Breakthrough Strategy for Total Quality, Productivity, and Competitiveness*. New York: McGraw-Hill, p. 16.

Imai, M. (1986). *Kaizen; The Key to Japan's Competitive Success*. Toronto: Random House.

Indy Quality, Productivity and Involvement Council. Donald R. Curtis, Executive Director, 9035 Pinecreek Court, Indianapolis, IN 46256, Tel: 317-845-4393.

Joiner, B. L. (1994). *Fourth Generation Management: The New Business Consciousness*. New York: McGraw-Hill, pp. 121–122.

Juran, J. M. (1988). *On Planning for Quality*. New York: Macmillan.

Kane, E. J. (1986). "IBM's Quality Focus on the Business Process." *Quality Progress*. April, pp. 24–33.

Schultz, L. E. (1994). *Profiles in Quality: Learning From The Masters*. White Plains, NY: Quality Resources.

Suzaki, K. (1994). *The New Manufacturing Challenge*. New York: The Free Press, p. 137.

Wheatley, M. (1994). "Can the U.S. Army Become a Learning Organization?" *Journal for Quality and Participation*. March, p. 52.

Chapter 2

THE BEST
KNOWN WAY

In this chapter, you will learn how process mastering puts people's creativity and energy to work. Process mastering is an outgrowth of the first stage of a five-stage plan for process improvement proposed by Peter Scholtes. His first stage is called "Understand the Process."

To truly understand a process, Scholtes says you must:

- Describe the process
- Identify customer needs and concerns
- Describe a standard process.

"The significance of all knowledge is for possible action. And the significance of common conception is for community of action. Congruity of behavior is the ultimate practical test of common undertaking."

C.I. Lewis

Before your team can make improvements, each member must thoroughly understand the process. To really know what is right and what is wrong with a process, you must answer three questions:

- How does the process currently work?
- What is it supposed to accomplish? (That is, how does the output relate to customer needs)?

- What is the current best-known way to carry out the process?

When employees doing the same work use the same procedures, product, or service, uniformity and predictability often increase dramatically.

What has been lacking in many organizational improvement systems has been a practical way to carry out the standardization of processes. What follows is a method that really works!

Definition: What is the **Best Known Way**?
It is the safest, easiest, simplest current way to get results that satisfy customer needs, the road map for everyone to follow until a better method is chosen.

Here's an example: Imagine you are traveling to visit Aunt Martha, off the main road and getting low on fuel. You left your old road map in the other car. So you stop to ask directions.

"Pardon me, sir, can you tell me the best way to get to Valley Hills?"

If you were speaking to the local character, "Old John," he might tell you to "keep goin' west, on up the road to Smoky's, then turn south on Route 66. Don't you pay any attention to the Valley Hills Road sign right after you turn on 66, because the Iron Wells Bridge is out. Just keep on going up 66 about 14 miles to the Red Fox Gas Emporium and turn right on County Road 450. Valley Hills is over the hill and across Fishback Creek. Watch out for the Bump sign after you cross the bridge. If you get close enough to read it, it'll be too late. Ivan Miller broke a shock absorber, when he hit that chuckhole doin' 40, yesterday."

What "Old John" has given you is the current Best Known Way over to Valley Hills. He gave you a route to follow, some helpful information to save you some driving time, and what might happen if you fail to slow down on the other side of the bridge. The way he told you to go is not the future best way, because the road crew is replacing the Iron Wells Bridge, and it will be four lanes wide next year. But, Old John's way is the best way to get there *today*.

Figure 3. Process mastering gets the best results if the order below is followed

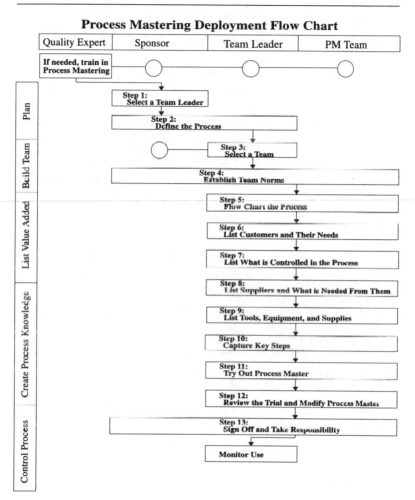

Process Mastering Deployment Flow Chart

Quality Expert	Sponsor	Team Leader	PM Team
If needed, train in Process Mastering	○	○	○

Plan

Step 1: Select a Team Leader

Step 2: Define the Process

Build Team

Step 3: Select a Team

Step 4: Establish Team Norms

List Value Added

Step 5: Flow Chart the Process

Step 6: List Customers and Their Needs

Step 7: List What is Controlled in the Process

Step 8: List Suppliers and What is Needed From Them

Create Process Knowledge

Step 9: List Tools, Equipment, and Supplies

Step 10: Capture Key Steps

Step 11: Try Out Process Master

Step 12: Review the Trial and Modify Process Master

Control Process

Step 13: Sign Off and Take Responsibility

Monitor Use

Maybe you know an Old John or Old Jane. The people who do the job are the process experts. They know the best route, even when it contradicts the formal maps. Process mastering provides a way to use Old John's know-how so that everyone benefits from his experience.

Process Mastering

Process mastering is taking command or control of a process. Joseph Juran says a process is "a systematic series of actions directed to the achievement of a goal." In other words, anything that you do the same way, time after time, to turn inputs into outputs—like completing expense reports, baking a pie, or taking a customer order over the phone, is a process.

Definition: A process is a sequential grouping of interrelated tasks, directed at producing one particular outcome.

We achieve process mastery by developing a process master that is basically a cookbook for doing the process—putting the Best Known Way down on paper. A completed process master covers all aspects of what it takes to control a process in a way that will achieve customer satisfaction. A process master is a document developed in a formal step-by-step method by the process experts, the people who do the work.

"Some people may be involved in a process because they perform a vital operation or task or have needed expertise. Others may be in the loop because they bear final responsibility for the outcomes."

C.J. McNair
Kathleen H.J. Leibfried

Step 1: Select a Team Leader

Development of a process master begins with the decision of a manager to sponsor a process master team. This person must have the authority, vision, and resources to support the team.

Figure 4. Step 1: Select a Team Leader

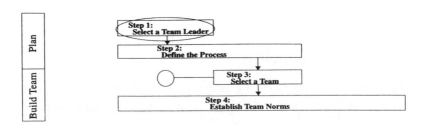

She or he is responsible for seeing that the team is trained in such things as process mastering, meeting skills, flow charting, and teamwork, and that the team has supplies, time, clerical support, and an area to meet. Finally, the sponsor must set any constraints or boundaries that may be necessary for the team. Refer to Team Chartering Checklist in Appendix B.

The first formal step in developing a process master is for the sponsor to select a team leader and to discuss the information mentioned in the paragraph above. Refer to Figures 3 and 4. The team leader is responsible for assembling the team, setting agendas, leading the meetings, and coordinating paperwork. The team leader is usually the work supervisor. This makes it easier to monitor the process to be sure everyone understands and follows the process master.

Team leaders should have:

- High energy and initiative
- The ability to use data
- Comfort with public speaking
- Empathy
- Respect of management
- The ability to manage meetings
- Knowledge
- Stability and maturity.

Definition: A **process master** is a document developed in a formal step-by-step method by the process experts—the people who do the work. It links customer needs, process controls, and supplier deliveries, so everyone will understand why and how to do the process steps, using the most effective current method.

The sponsor helps the team leader set process boundaries and meets with the team leader often enough to help the team through sticky spots along the way. The sponsor usually meets

Figure 5. Step 2: Define the Process

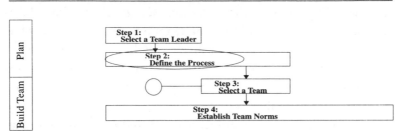

with the team at Step 4, to help set the team norms, and at Step 13 to sign off with the team. The main responsibility of the sponsor is to be a tie to management.

Step 2: Define the Process

The team leader and sponsor get together before the first team meeting and set process boundaries (Fig. 6). They should be careful to use any existing documents, such as Equipment Manuals, Standard Operating Procedures, and Safety Manuals to save time and to take advantage of previous work. They should be guided by Scholtes' questions:

- Precisely where does the process you are going to study start and stop?
- What inputs and suppliers are part of this process?
- What are its outputs (products or services)?
- Who are the internal customers of this output?
- Who will purchase the product or service?
- Who will use the product or service? (These are not always the same people.)

It is usually helpful to walk or think through the operation and note natural breaks between processes. An example of the start of a process might be where a person acquires work to be done. This might be when the customer service representative picks up the phone to take an order. A natural break is often found where work is transferred between departments. One example is where canned foods exit the cook room to be

Figure 6. Picture of a Process

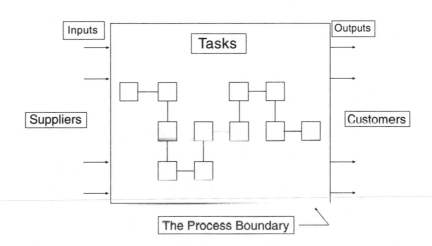

labeled. Another break is after molded reflector lenses are finished on their way to assembly.

Processes that are too large will take too long to finish. A process should be of a size that can be mastered in about six to eight team meetings of 45 minutes each. An example of a process that would take a long time to finish is "Operation of the zoo." Processes that are too trivial will waste your time. An example of a trivial process would be punching tickets at the admission gate. A process that could be mastered in six to eight meetings is ordering zoo supplies.

Step 3: Select a Team

The sponsor and team leader list the people who work with the process. Scholtes recommends up to five process workers be on

Figure 7. Step 3: Select a Team

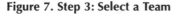

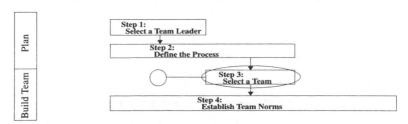

the team. This is in addition to the sponsor and team leader. Temporary team members with special expertise may be invited to attend only one or two meetings to help everyone understand process fundamentals. Remember, the time to reach consensus grows exponentially with growth of the number of people in the room. More people slow down the process. On the other hand, the more people you have on the team, the easier it will be for the work group to accept the master. In a union environment, it is best for the union leaders to be part of the planning process to gain their support.

You must consider several things when selecting team members. The team needs to have know-how, including a clear understanding of the tricks of the trade. This means Old John needs to contribute his experience and short cuts. New or inexperienced workers can contribute by asking questions and talking about how they do the job. All work shifts need to be considered. Most of the friction that develops between shifts comes from misunderstanding shift-change responsibilities. One way for different shifts to meet is at shift changes. Rotation of meeting times may be necessary for all shifts to be able to attend. If you choose this rotation, some of the members will miss some of the meetings. They will need to be updated by the members in attendance. This is especially important in a three-shift operation.

There are several ways team members have been selected in actual practice.

- The natural work group could select up to five members to be on the team. In this scenario, the natural leaders of the work group are usually picked, leading to open communications and buy-in from those not on the team.

- Another way is for the team leader to pick people with different skill levels, ages, work locations, shifts, personal strengths, and educational backgrounds, to get as diverse a group as possible. This approach serves to get a cross-section, leading to buy-in from different segments of the work group.

- Team members rotate as process master teams come and go, so everyone helps periodically on a team. This method allows everyone to participate and keep their meeting skills sharp.

To help everyone understand process theory, someone from engineering, research, or the safety committee can be invited to one or two meetings to explain why parts of the process must be done only one way. For example, a microbiologist was invited to one meeting to discuss food spoilage and the reasons for "breaking down" a pump during equipment cleanup.

In smaller companies, suppliers are often called upon for their expertise. For example, a small printing company asks their ink supplier to help them standardize press setups.

The chosen team members need to be willing and able to learn the basic principles underlying their process. They also need to be willing and capable of communicating and involving other members from the natural work groups who are not on the team. They need to keep the rest of the workers informed about what is being discussed in the team meetings. They need to get input from other workers on methods and safety hazards, and they should look for opportunities to solicit special help to draw flow charts and graphics. This will result in better buy-in from all the workers when the process master paperwork is done. This also levels the workload and speeds up completion.

Step 4: Establish Team Norms

A norm is a standard, model, or pattern regarded as typical for a specific group. All groups have them. According to

Figure 8. Step 4: Establish Team Norms

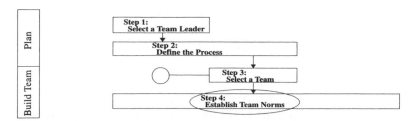

Henderson et al., norms may be imposed by outside authority, from cultural patterns or by the group itself. They are limits by which members must conform in order to be part of the team, such as attendance, confidentiality, and punctuality. Norms are behavior patterns that are highly valued or desirable to the team, such as honesty, sharing, being supportive, politeness, and no put-downs. They include agreed-upon decision-making methods such as voting or consensus.

It is very important for a new process mastering team to take the time to write down their norms because the team will be much more efficient in the long run. It is simply a matter of everyone having the opportunity to suggest and agree upon how the group will work together. It is important to write the norms down (ideally in a positive tone), and provide each person with a copy for future reference. It is acceptable to challenge and add to the list at any time. It is expected that any member of the team will eagerly point out when he or she feels someone or the team has violated a norm.

Figure 9. Sample Team Norms

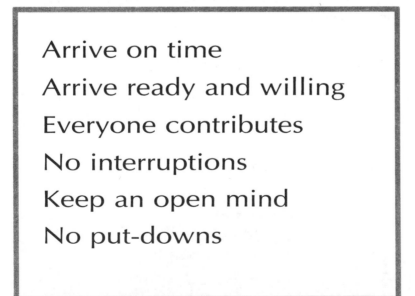

Arrive on time

Arrive ready and willing

Everyone contributes

No interruptions

Keep an open mind

No put-downs

In addition to the example norms listed in Figure 9, very basic points must be agreed upon:

- Standard time the team will meet, e.g., day of the week and time of day
- Length of the meeting, e.g., 45 minutes
- Location of meeting
- Who will keep notes
- Person responsible for meeting supplies and equipment
- Accommodation of different shifts.

Establishing norms may seem tedious and unnecessary, especially for people who work together day in and day out; however, experience has proven that this is a good investment in time.

Step 5: Flow Chart the Process

We are now at Step 5 in the Creating a Process Master flowchart (Fig. 10). We have included a process master written about grocery shopping. We chose to include an easy example that is familiar to everyone. We will refer to the grocery shopping example throughout Chapter 2. In addition, we will cite "real world" examples to help you see the points as we go.

At this step in doing a process master, you will begin to discover the confusion and variance that occurs in every process that involves people. This is where the team discusses and decides upon the sequence of tasks that is best for doing the process under study. If you are alert, you will discover extra work that you may have been doing for years that was unnec-

Figure 10. Step 5: Flow Chart the Process

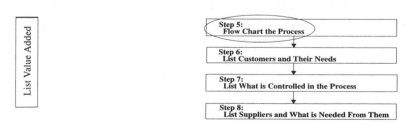

Figure 11. Example of a Top Down Flow Chart Layout

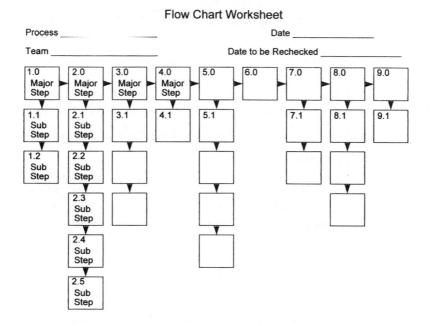

essary or even harmful. *The "best known way" is one of the ways the tasks are being done now and that the team can agree is the best.* You will learn the "best known way" as determined by the collective wisdom and experience in the room.

Parking Lot List: This type of list is often called a "parking lot" because it lets you save valuable thoughts for later consideration without taking the team's time by discussing each idea when it arises. Stay on track and use the parking lot frequently.

At this point, it is necessary to caution everyone not to get into a creative mood, that is, don't dream up possible new and better ways to do the process. Ideas will surely surface about how the process might be done better. Collect these ideas on a parking lot list for later use, but don't be tempted to write them into the master before the existing process is fully defined and stabilized.

Flow charting the process requires that you divide the process into sequential steps to identify the actual path that a product or service follows in the process.

We will use the top-down flowchart as shown in Figure 11. After you have determined the process boundaries as we discussed earlier, it is usually best to try to identify the major or most basic steps first. For scheduling reasons, no more than six to nine major steps should be considered. This forces the team members to sort and focus their thinking on only the essential major steps. If significantly more major steps are identified, the team may wish to reduce the size of the process under consideration or be alert for opportunities to combine some of the major steps.

> "It is neither possible or necessary to standardize all operations. However, the critical elements...should be measurable and standardized."
>
> Masaaki Imai

Figure 12. One family's top down flow chart for grocery shopping

Flow Chart Worksheet

Process   Grocery Shopping   Date _____ March 7, 1998

Team ____ The Wilsons _____   Date to be Rechecked _____ March 1999

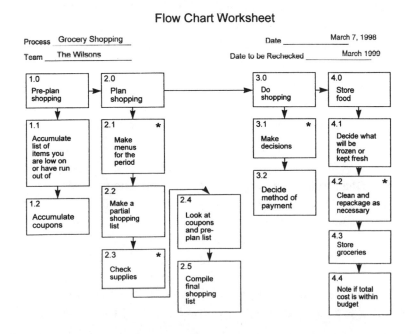

Figure 13. Step 6: List Customers and Their Needs

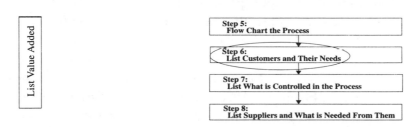

Since development of the flowchart is rather fluid at first, some people find it efficient to write the individual steps on sticky notes so they can be easily replaced or moved around.

Following the listing of the major steps across the top of the paper or flip chart, begin listing the substeps below each major step. Realize that you are agreeing to do each substep, one after another under major step 1.0, before proceeding to do the steps under major step 2.0. We recommend that all steps be numbered as shown in Figure 12 and that the name of the process step begins with an action verb, for example, "adjust temperature" not "temperature adjustment."

As the team discusses and decides on the steps and their sequence, differences of opinion and experience will surface. This is when the collective judgment and synergy of the team will come into play. It may be necessary to actually go back to the work site to study and observe before deciding what is the "best known way."

Step 6: List the Customers' Needs and Process Interactions

Definition: An **external customer** is anyone outside the organization who receives its products, services, or knowledge. Commonly, external customers are the ones who pay the bills, although regulatory departments like the IRS are sometimes included.

The process mastering team should list the customers of the process and their most important needs. Juran suggests fol-

Figure 14. External Customer "A" Chart is used to identify external customer needs and how they are met

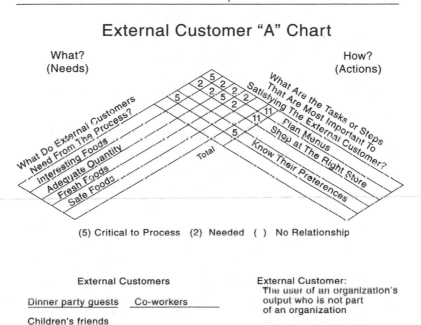

External Customer "A" Chart

(5) Critical to Process   (2) Needed   ( ) No Relationship

External Customers		External Customer:
Dinner party guests	Co-workers	The user of an organization's output who is not part of an organization
Children's friends		

lowing the product to see whom it impacts. *Anyone* impacted by the product is a *customer*. It is very important to list external customers. This step helps workers to see both a wider picture and how their output is used. It also shows where gaps may exist between needed and actual performance.

Not everyone has contact with an external customer, but nearly everyone does something that is ultimately seen outside the organization. There may be exceptions, but you should be aware of who your external customers are and what they need. An external customer of the accounting department may be an auditor, bank, or even the Internal Revenue Service.

A complete list of every single external customer is not necessary. If you have too many customers to list, try to list classes of customers. Juran suggests listing the "vital few customers" that cover most of the customer categories. An example of the classes of customers visiting a theme park might include grouping by age or by gender. Identify the one or two customer groups it is most important to satisfy.

To begin, in our example we listed the external customers for the grocery shopping process. They are "dinner party guests," "children's friends," and "co-workers." Cookies are for the Wednesday A.M. coffee break. You may refer to Figure 14 and follow it as we explain the example.

In real life, you will need to list your vital customers or customer groups. Then, you will need to list the needs of these vital customers.

A representative of these customers could be invited to be part of this process. Someone from sales or customer service—with close customer contact—can give the team valuable advice. The team and customer representative should prioritize the two to five most important customer needs. You will use the process mastering "A" chart (see Fig. 14) to compare needs to actions (we call it an "A" chart because of the shape).

This is done quickly by having the team brainstorm external customer needs and writing them on the left side ("what" side) of an "A" chart. An "A" chart drawn on a flip chart makes this visible to the entire team.

Customers' needs should be objectively defined. That is, they should be written so everyone understands the meaning clearly. In writing definitions, avoid vague words like "on time," "mostly," "usually," "hot," and "finished." Better definitions look like this:

- Car ready for pickup at time promised
- All parts included in package
- Parts are fired at 500°F for 60–65 minutes
- Tires are inflated to 32 psi.

These needs should be as measurable as possible. NOTE: Don't forget to list any safety concerns as customer needs.

In the case of the grocery shopping example, the external customers' needs are:

- Interesting food
- Adequate quantity
- Fresh food
- Safe food.

Then, the team brainstorms the most important steps or tasks that contribute to customer satisfaction. These steps are recorded on the right side of the "A" chart. Look at your process and list the actions within the process that affect how the customers' needs are met. List the most important two to five actions or tasks taken in the process to keep the customer satisfied. Write the action steps in the external customer "A" chart on the right side ("how" side). Refer to the example for the process of grocery shopping, shown in Figure 14.

For grocery shopping, the most important tasks are:

- Plan menus

- Shop at right store

- Know their preferences.

The point of this procedure is to help the team discover which tasks or actions in the process are most critical to a successful outcome—customer satisfaction. To reach a conclusion, values are placed in the boxes at the peak of the "A" based on how strong an action or task impacts the customers' needs. The number 5 indicates a strong impact, while the number 2 indicates a relationship, but not a strong factor. A blank indicates no relationship between the action or task and the customers' needs. To accomplish this, it is often helpful to take the action listed and put it in the form of a question beginning with the word "how." As an example, *"How strongly does 'planning menus' affect the first customers' need—'interesting food'?"* Our conclusion is that this is a strong relationship. So we put a 5 in the top box.

Continuing—"How strongly does 'planning menus' affect 'adequate quantity'?" We felt it was *needed* but not critical to the external customers. Therefore, we put a 2 in the next box. "How does 'planning menus' affect 'fresh food'?" We said it was *needed* and gave it a 2. "How does 'planning menus' affect 'safe food'?" Again we chose *needed* and inserted a 2 in the box. Follow this same procedure for "shops at right store" and "know their preferences."

After this procedure is complete for all the actions, find totals for each action. In the example in Figure 14, we found two actions to be equally important. Sometimes one action will be clearly more important. Other times, as in this example, there will be ties. The results from completing the "A" chart are clues to the team about the importance of various steps in the process. What is most important to customer satisfaction may need to be routinely measured. This also may be a starting point for a quality improvement effort.

Definition: Internal customers are the people to whom you give work, products, services, or information within the organization.

Internal customers include the people who work in the next process—your supervisor and his boss. You are the customer of the people in the upstream process and internal service departments like purchasing and payroll. You are your supervisor's customer when she works to get you a raise. The team should list its internal customers. Identify the two or three most important customers to satisfy. In our grocery shopping example, our internal customers are: spouse, children, a live-in relative, and our cats (Fig. 15). List the needs of these vital few customers. A representative of these customers could be invited to help out with this process. List your internal customers' two to five most important needs. These needs should be described in concrete, measurable terms if possible. Here are some examples from past teams:

- Pallet tickets attached at lower right corner of each side of pallet

- Requisitions completely filled in, signed by supervisor

- Computer files updated and backed up before midnight every work day

- Trucks hooked to docks and chocked before lift truck enters.

Write the internal customer needs under the "what" side of the customer "A" chart. NOTE: Don't forget to list any safety concerns as customer needs. Look at the process and discuss the tasks or actions that affect how the customers' needs are met.

Figure 15. Internal Customer "A" Chart is used to identify internal customer needs and how they are met

Internal Customer "A" Chart

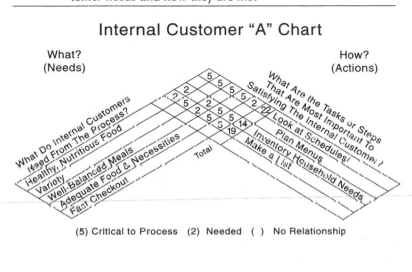

What? (Needs)   How? (Actions)

(5) Critical to Process   (2) Needed   ( ) No Relationship

Internal Customers		Internal Customer:
Spouse	Live-in relative	The people to whom you give work, products, services, or information within the organization
Children	Cats	

List the most important two to five actions taken to keep the customer satisfied. Write them on the "how" side of the internal customer "A" chart. Compare the actions in the process to the needs of the customer as explained above in the section on external customers.

The most important action step(s) that result from the analysis will indicate what tasks in the process are most important to the internal customer. The team must keep the results in mind when choosing measurements of process quality.

Step 7: List What Is Controlled in the Process

The team should list items they watch, do, or control in their process on the "what" side of the process "A" chart. Please note that in this part of the process evaluation, people sometimes get confused between the "whats" and the "hows."

Figure 16. Step 7: List what is controlled in the process

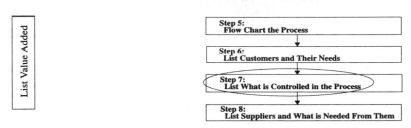

Refer to the grocery example in Figure 17. For the "what" side of the "A" chart, the team should simply make a list of what they do and/or have discretion over in the process. Use your judgment in deciding on critical conditions and control points within the process. These are parts of the process where things could go wrong, causing rework or customer problems. They could include places where measurements are currently being checked.

Figure 17. The Control "A" chart shows steps that can be controlled and how they are measured

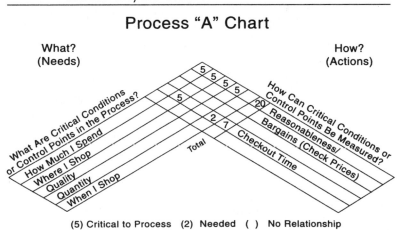

Examples of Critical Conditions

Control Points	Typical Measurements
Machining a shaft	Shaft diameter
Wastewater cleanup	Biochemical oxygen demand
Cereal box filling	Fill weight
Molded part shape	Mold temperature
Cash flow	Days receivable
Order turnaround time	% On-time incoming shipments
Color matching	Meter calibration

On the "how" side of the "A" chart, the team should concentrate on how critical conditions or control points in the process can be measured. Suzaki explains control points this way. "Just as we may frequently check car speed, our location on the map, or fuel level during a trip, we should practice a similar concept when running a company or a mini-company... even if we know the destination and chart the course, without an adequate monitoring and feedback system we may lose our way."

The importance of the control points on the "how" side should be evaluated against what is watched on the "what" side of the "A." Place a number in the measurement box corresponding to each control point. Total the measurement rows and decide which one or two measurements are most critical to the successful outcome of the process. This information will be helpful in deciding on key steps later. Refer to Step 10 of "Creating a Process Master."

Figure 18. Step 8: List suppliers and what is needed from them

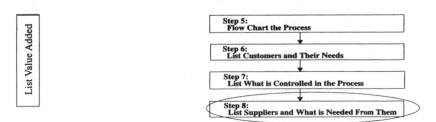

Step 8: List Needs From Suppliers and How They Will Be Used

Definition: A **supplier** is anyone providing products, services, or knowledge to a process. Internal suppliers are usually upstream from the process. External suppliers are outside the organization.

Next, the team should list its suppliers and list what is needed from them. This set of needs describes characteristics that the team finds indispensable in doing its job. Please refer to Figure 19.

Some examples will help to clarify this step:

- Truckloads of milk arrive between 8:00 A.M. and noon

- Computer stays "UP" between 6:00 A.M. and midnight

- Automated teller is refilled with cash before every three-day weekend

Write the most important two to five needs on the "what" side of the supplier "A" chart. On the "how" side, write in how the process uses what the supplier delivers. For the above needs, here are our examples:

- Milk is stowed before truck debarks at 4:00 P.M.

- Computer is required all day to input orders

- Cash is always available to customers.

See Figure 19 for grocery shopping "A" chart.

Because you will be looking upstream toward the suppliers, the question to ask should be focused upstream. This is opposite of the downstream focus of the other "A" charts. The supplier question is focused on the use to be made of their deliveries. For example: "How important is the ("how side" entry) to the ("what side" entry)? Complete the numerical boxes at the peak of the "A" in order to understand and judge the most important supplier outputs, as compared to the actions taken in your process.

Figure 19. The Supplier "A" chart shows what is needed to carry out the process and how your suppliers' deliveries are used in the process

Supplier "A" Chart

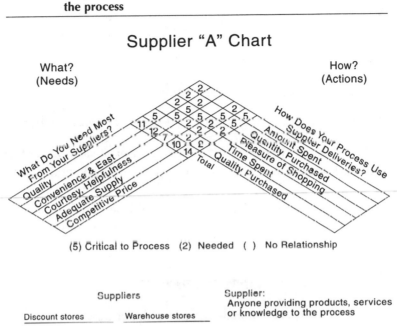

What? (Needs)

How? (Actions)

(5) Critical to Process   (2) Needed   ( ) No Relationship

Suppliers

Discount stores   Warehouse stores

General grocery stores   Wholesale clubs

Supplier:
Anyone providing products, services or knowledge to the process

Step 9: List Tools, Equipment, and Supplies

Process Master:
Grocery Shopping

Tools, equipment, and supplies:
- Cash/checkbook/charge cards
- Shopping list
- Calculator
- Coupons
- Bags, if needed.

At this point, the team should list the tools, equipment, and supplies that are required to complete the process being analyzed. Some judgment is required as to the extent of equipment to list. As an example, you would not bother listing lights, a

Figure 20. Step 9: List tools, equipment, and supplies

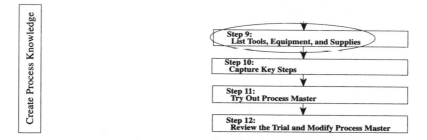

sink, or table if they are bolted down and/or always present in the work area. On the other hand, portable tools and equipment that need to be in perfect operating condition, or are essential to complete the process, should be listed. It should also be noted if inspection, calibration, or maintenance is required before use in the process.

Process Master:

Inspect and maintain fire extinguishers

Tools, equipment, and supplies:

- Silicone spray or grease

- Dry chemical AB

- Inspection tags.

In the area of supplies, there could be some confusion or overlap with what this process passes along to the customer in the form of added value. What should be listed here are the consumable items that are not a readily identifiable part of the process output that the customer sees. See above for examples.

One of the finer points to consider when listing tools, equipment, and supplies is to be specific if it is appropriate. This could be as vague as a "clean" bucket or "extra long" tie wire or as specific as a 150 foot-pound torque wrench or an organic vapor/high efficiency respirator. Take advantage of this discussion to establish what tool, equipment, or supply works best even to the point of establishing brand name and supplier, if this will reduce variation in your process.

Figure 21. Step 10: Capture Key Steps

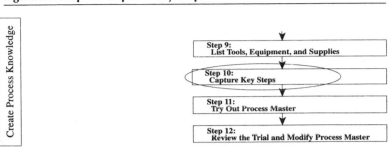

One final thought is appropriate to help establish the importance of this step in doing a process master. Often, process masters are developed for processes that are done infrequently or only in emergencies. Nothing can be much worse than being a long way from home base or being in the middle of a repair job when you discover you don't have everything you need. This listing of tools, equipment, and supplies can serve as a checklist to assure that everything required for a process is available before it is begun.

Step 10: Capture Key Steps

As you have worked through the flow chart, it may have become apparent that some process steps are more important than others—for various reasons. Not all steps in the process must be done the "best known way" in order to have a successful outcome. Only those steps that are key or critical need to be standardized. In order to select the key steps, these six questions should be asked:

1. Have errors happened because the step is too complicated?

2. Are there safety concerns or hazards present in the step?

3. Is it a production start-up or shut-down step?

4. Has the step been found to be critical to the internal or external customers?

Figure 22. The team uses the Key Step Worksheet to capture The Best Known Way

Process Mastering
Key Step Worksheet

Process: _____   Date: _____

Team Name: _____   Date to be Rechecked: _____

Key Step #	Key Step Name (Starts With a Verb)	Best Known Way	Tricks of The Trade	Consequences of Doing It Wrong

Handling Exceptions				

Process Measurements	What is Measured	How it is Measured	Target	Range

5. Is it necessary or desirable to have a control point at the end of the step where you can measure things such as quantity, cost, timeliness, accuracy, function, service-ability, aesthetics, or dimensions?

6. Do the numbers in the "A" charts indicate this step is critical to meeting customer needs?

Figure 23. Key Step Worksheet for grocery shopping example

Process Mastering
Key Step Worksheet

Process: ___Grocery Shopping___   Date: _____March 15, 1998_____

Team Name: ____The Wilsons____   Date to be Rechecked: _March, 1999_

Key Step	Key Step Name (Starts With a Verb)	Best Known Way	Tricks of The Trade	Consequences of Doing It Wrong
2.1	Make menus for the period	1. Look at family schedule to find lunch and dinner needs. 2. Check freezer, refrigerator, and pantry to see what is available and should/could be used. 3. Make menus for the meals.		May purchase items you don't need—that may spoil. May have to make another trip to the store. Not as much flexibility. More stress. Disappointment.
2.3	Check Supplies	1. Check shelves to see if you have necessary ingredients. 2. Check supplies of staples. 3. Look for cleaning supply needs.		You will forget something you need.
3.1	Make Decisions	1. Decide on produce based on price quality and availability. 2. If price is very favorable and it can be stored, purchase items not on list.	Compare $/unit of competing brands. Flexible to take advantage of sales. If price is too high, don't buy even if there is a coupon. Check items off of the list as they are chosen.	Bill goes up. Food is wasted. Don't have what you need.

Handling Exceptions	When the store is out of a particular herb or spice, substitute something similar.			
Process Measurements	What Is Measured	How It Is Measured	Target	Range
	Cost	Receipt	Budget	6 10%

If the answer is yes to any of the questions, the step should be considered key to the successful outcome of the process. It should be starred on the flowchart (see Fig. 12) and analyzed on the key step worksheet. We suggest that a team complete the form row by row, rather than column by column.

Begin by filling out the blanks at the top of the key step worksheet: Process Name, Team Name, Date, and Date to be Rechecked. The blanks in the first two columns, Key Step # and Key Step Name are simply lifted from the starred boxes on the flow chart. See Figure 23 for grocery shopping example.

The "best known way" column is filled in after the team has agreed on the best standard way this step is now done. The "best known way" blank can be completed in words. A sketch or an annotated photograph, however, will convey the standard method more clearly and succinctly. Some organizations are using digital cameras to take digital photographs of the key steps. They then download the picture to a personal computer where it can be edited, formatted, and imported into the process master document.

Use of the "tricks of the trade" column is optional, in that after completing the "best known way" blank, there may be no further explanation required. However, wisdom among the workers should not be lost or overlooked. Take advantage of this opportunity to catalog this wisdom. Also, this is the place where any safety alert should be recorded. We cannot over-stress this point! It is one thing to have a less-than-perfect process, but it is another thing altogether to allow a process to operate that can hurt someone or that may harm the environment. See "Safety and Process Mastering" in Chapter 6.

When completing the final column, Consequences of Doing It Wrong, some of the answers will be straightforward and blatantly obvious. Often, however, the team will for the first time see the wider consequences of doing a step wrong or unsafely. This is one of those subtle "ah ha's" that make process mastering so rewarding to the organization and the workers.

Near the bottom of the form is a blank for handling exceptions. It is primarily intended to elicit discussion and agreement on how to handle exceptions that may be encountered. The team should write in exceptional problems that have happened in the past and could be expected to happen again. For example, dry ice cream stabilizer usually arrives in 50-pound bags. The bags are lifted by hand to the top of a blender, the bag is opened, and all 50 pounds are poured in. Twice in the past year, the supplier has sent stabilizer in 300-pound drums. Both times, the operator used a scoop to weigh the 50 pounds and transfer it into the blender.

The appropriate key step worksheet entry would look like this: "If supplier sends stabilizer in drums, weigh and transfer it with a scoop."

For other, unpredictable exceptions, this blanket statement is acceptable: "If you cannot follow the process master, check with supervisor and/or fill out Exception form."

The final section deals with process measurements. As mentioned elsewhere, it is very important that each process has at least one point of measurement.

Figure 24. Step 11: Try out Process Master

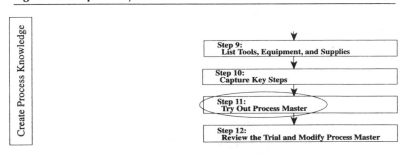

It is frequently difficult for teams to find and choose an appropriate and effective measurement for a process. We're not sure of the reason for this. We suspect that it is a mental block associated with: "You mean we have to take a measurement and record it every time we do this?" Or, "If we have this data, it may tell people something we don't want them to know." The discussion of measurements may be kicked off with this question to the team: What should we measure in this process that will give us the most information on how to make it better? Keep in mind that it is the process that is being measured, not the people within it. Having a section to fill in at the bottom of the Key Step Worksheet encourages the team to discuss and decide on at least one important measurement that will serve as a report card on the health of the process.

Step 11: Try Out the Process Master

Now it is time to try out the process master (see Fig. 24). It is especially important for everyone who works in the process to try following each process step. Of course, those who helped write it will need little or no training. Others who were not on the team will need to be trained. The supervisor or team leader should lead or participate in the training of additional employees, to be sure they understand the "best known way" defined by the team.

A trial period should be long enough that everyone has a chance to try the process master several times. It is also good to have a novice do the work following the process master to

Figure 25. Step 12: Review the trial and modify Process Master

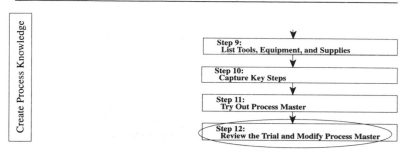

see if it makes sense. The management sponsor is often far enough from the process that he or she can serve as the novice or guinea pig! This is a critical time. The supervisor of the process must take an intense interest in observing and encouraging every worker to follow the steps outlined in the process master. This is the time when deficiencies or "over standardization" in the process master will show up. It is also a time when old, comfortable habits will be challenged, and it will become apparent if there is a supportive, learning atmosphere present in the department or organization. All experiences, exceptions, and suggestions should be collected and written down for the team's use in finishing the first generation of the process master.

There are no perfect process masters. The first one a team does is not as polished as the second one. The process is what needs to be understood. The way a process master looks is secondary to what it teaches the team about the process.

Step 12: Review the Trial and Modify Process Master

After the trial is complete, the team members should discuss how it went (see Fig. 25). The team should cover these points:

- Are there any steps, tricks of the trade, or safety concerns missing, inaccurate, or unclear?

- Should any exceptions encountered during the trial be included in the master?

Figure 26. Step 13: Sign off and take responsibility

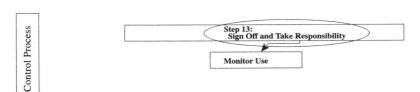

- Has the management sponsor of the team or another novice worked through the process, following the master, to find anything that doesn't make sense?

The mastery team needs to compare the process flow and all of the process master documents, to be sure nothing was left out. Now is the time to modify the process master, if needed. The process master may need minor surgery to correct any flaws. It is also the time for any final details to be worked out, before word processing the documents. And, by the way, the typist should code each version of the documents to allow for easy updating and reference.

After the discussion is over and the decisions are made, the document should be put in final form—organized and typed in a way that is clear and easy to follow. Note, there is a danger here. There is a tendency at this point to consider the master complete. Everyone needs to be reminded that this is a living document, and it should be challenged and revised continually.

Step 13: Complete and Sign Off

The cover page of the completed process master is a very important part of the document (see Fig. 26). We suggest that an organization have a standard format that includes at least the following items:

- Number (a uniform numbering scheme should be followed)

- Name of the process master

- Date first completed

Figure 27. Sample cover page for Process Master

Process Master Sign-Off Sheet

Process Master Number: _____

Process Name: _____

Date: _____

> Our process master team has identified and written down the best known ways to carry out our process. By signing below, I agree to follow the attached process master whenever possible. I understand that exceptional situations may force a temporary change in the process. When this happens, I will act in the best interests of my customers. I will also turn in a Process Master Exception Report of the temporary changes for possible updating of the process master.

Team Sponsor: _____

Team Leader: _____

Process Team Members:

_____   _____

_____   _____

_____   _____

_____   _____

Dates of Revisions: _____

_____

_____

_____

_____

Figure 28. The use of the Process Master requires monitoring

- Management sponsor—signature
- Team leader/process owner—signature
- Process workers—signatures
- Date of revisions and/or date of scheduled review.

We believe that when people sign the document they created, they are attesting to the fact that it is their best work, that they will stand by it, and that they will use, support, and take responsibility for it (see Fig. 27 for sample cover sheet).

Monitor Use

Now that you have it, what do you do with it (see Fig. 28)? The master is done. It is all typed up with signatures on the cover page. Now what? It depends. One thing is for sure: you cannot simply check it off the "to do" list, put it in a file drawer, and go back to business as usual. Traditional SOPs suffer the "file drawer burial." This could be the worst mistake you can make. If the process was important enough to spend the time and effort to complete a master of it, you better use it. If you don't, not only will you not benefit from the work you did, but you will get less enthusiasm and lower quality work from the next team you ask to do a process master.

Exactly what you do with the hard copy of the process master does depend on your situation. Of the process masters we have seen completed, nearly all have been posted in the work area to remind everyone of the "best known way." This also helped to communicate with suppliers and customers. If a master was developed for a process that is done daily, the pages could be put in a workers' notebook inside plastic sleeves to be available as needed. It could be put under glass or a desk or counter top. If the process is in a damp area, the process master can be laminated for protection. If the master was developed for a process that is used infrequently, it could be put into a notebook to be reviewed each time before the process is carried out. Some processes require data gathering on a periodic basis. The check sheet or data sheet can be housed in a notebook with the process master. Additionally, some processes require access to government regulations. These could be combined into a single document or notebook. Of course, more and more, process masters can be distributed on intranets. The benefits are obvious: the masters are immediately accessible in their most recent form, the need to store and ascertain paper documents is eliminated, and distribution is efficient and simultaneous.

In any case, remember that the process master is a living document. It cannot simply be put on the shelf and forgotten. It is simply the beginning, the stable foundation to launch a continuous improvement effort on the process. The supervisor of the process must lead in the process master's implementation. However, everyone within the process must see to it that the document is followed and maintained. And the supervisor must see to it that the master is challenged and continuously updated if the process is to improve.

Start and Continue Measurements

Measurements should start as soon as the team leader sees that everyone is following the process master. Twenty to twenty-five data points should be graphed to show any trends or gaps between needed and actual performance before trying any changes to the process.

It is important to establish a procedure for taking measurements. Agree on such things as who, when, and how the measurements or data will be gathered and displayed. When a stable method for data gathering is established, you can have more confidence you are actually measuring what is happening in the process and not variation in data gathering.

Exceptions to the Process Master

The plan is that when a process master is complete, there is one "best known way" to do the process. Experience tells us, however, that everything doesn't always go as planned. Occasionally, a piece of equipment will break down, a government inspector will change criteria, a supplier will change package size, etc. When an exception happens, it should be documented by listing the reason for the exception, the action that was taken, the result, who made the exception, and the date of occurrence. This information should be stored with the process master. The process owner (team leader) should take responsibility for accumulating these exceptional happenings. The leader should also be responsible for challenging the continuation of exceptions because they tend to become permanent. And if they are permanent, then the master should be revised. See Process Exception Report Form in Appendix A.

The work team should meet periodically to review exceptions and to consider the list of "parking lot ideas" (ideas and suggestions accumulated over time). Ideas should focus on quality, cost, delivery, safety, speed, and morale issues. It is also important to reduce complexity, the variation caused by excessive process steps. The ideas should be tried one at a time, on a small scale, to see the effect. Measurement data should be compared before and after the change. The idea is that work should be accepted on a consensus basis by the work team. Standardize the changes that make the process better.

Make It Better

You now have established the "best known way" to do a particular process. There are two rules incumbent on everyone involved.

RULE ONE

Everyone must follow the process as described. Supervisors and workers must insist on this!

Rule Two

Everyone must be constantly looking for ways to improve the process. Ideas should be gathered. Tests should be run. And when the results warrant it, the process should be changed and improved.

References

Henderson, R., J. Kirby, J. Mullen, and S. Whitaker. (1994). *Advanced Facilitator Course Trainer Guide*. Indianapolis: Indy Quality, Productivity and Involvement Council, Inc., Draft, p. 8.

Imai, M. (1986). *Kaizen; The Key to Japan's Competitive Success*. Toronto: Random House.

Juran, J. M. (1988). *Juran on Planning for Quality*. New York: Macmillan, pp. 27–29.

Lewis, C. I. (1956). *Mind and the World-Order; Outline of a Theory of Knowledge*. New York: Dover, p. 90.

McNair, C. J. and K. H. J. Leibfried. (1992). *Benchmarking—A Tool for Continuous Improvement*. New York: HarperBusiness, p. 55.

Scholtes, P. (1988). *The Team Handbook*. Madison, WI: Joiner Associates, Chapter 3, p. 18.

Suzaki, K. (1989). *The New Shop-Floor Challenge*. New York: The Free Press, p. 240.

Chapter 3

MANAGEMENT'S ROLE

Justification and Decision

Managers face a jungle of priorities, goals, and strategies. The decision of which resources to place in the most promising areas can be frustrating. Competing actions can suboptimize the system. Processes should be analyzed to see if they contribute to meeting customer needs.

Ineffective business processes cost U.S. businesses billions of dollars every year, according to Harrington. He notes that between 40 and 70 percent of the white-collar effort adds no value, and that customers are five times more apt to turn away from you because of poor business processes than poor products.

Many companies have tried to quantify the improvement in profits that resulted from training of their managers and workers. One automotive company source says that applied training costs are returned 100-fold. Another survey of executives reports

"Everything we do today can be done better by concentrating on the process...let's give our employees a fair chance at success by starting business process improvement activities today."

H.J. Harrington

"If management cannot get people to follow the established rules and standards, nothing else it does will matter."

Masaaki Imai

"It is not enough to manage results. The way in which those results are achieved (the process) is also important. If we _are_ achieving the results, we need to know why. If we are _not_ achieving the results, we need to know why. In both cases, to a great degree, the answer lies in the process."

Geary A. Rummler
Alan P. Brache

that applied training costs pay back in two months or less in increased productivity and morale improvement. Whatever the ratio, the investment in process mastering training and implementation pays immediate dividends on the investment. Variable costs will decrease. Productivity will increase through increasing throughput, less waste, and uniform products and services.

There are numerous reasons to do process mastering. In Japan, companies typically devote two-thirds of their R & D budget to *process design* and one-third to *product design*. In the U.S. companies spend just the opposite. This focus on processes results in far fewer defects and related costs for early production runs, and the few defects that do appear are corrected much quicker, improving product reliability significantly.

Common wisdom in the quality professions is that 30 percent of everyone's job is associated with rework. It costs ten times more to regain a customer than to keep one. It costs ten times more to return an incorrect or damaged product to a supplier than it does to ship it right the first time. The average readily identifiable cost for an arm fracture is $10,000 and for an on-the-job death is $1,000,000. Experts suggest that the real or total cost for an accident is four to five times the easily identified costs. These are actual costs you can measure. What about your reputation? What about the emotional cost to your employees or volunteers? Obviously, anything that can be done to reduce the costs associated with these types of wastes would be worthwhile.

Another reason to employ process mastering is to model processes that have never been done before. This disciplined technique guides a team through a systematic approach that makes sure the concerns of all stakeholders of the process are addressed.

Perhaps the simplest but most compelling reason to do process mastering is to reduce variation. Some might refer to this as bringing stability. Money is always saved and customers are always better served when the outcomes from processes are predictable and the variations are small. Predictable processes make scheduling easier and help to smooth out work flow without employing excess workers.

Management must make the decision whether one or more of these reasons is worth the investment of time, money, and attention. Our experience says it is. We've never seen a situation where a group of workers wasn't able to make a significant contribution that paid back the investment many times over. If you've come to the same conclusion, you must decide how to proceed.

Deployment of Process Mastering

Deployment will depend on your situation, culture, approach, and organizational experience to date.

If process mastering is new to the organization, the intent and reasons for the effort must be communicated to everyone. The intent to improve customer satisfaction will be supported by focusing on reducing variation in the processes that affect customers most directly.

The rollout of process mastering to the organization could be done in each department or in a large meeting. The intent should be to help satisfy the customers through use of uniform methods wherever the method is important.

Training must be provided to those who will be involved. This can be done in a training class using general examples, or it can be done just-in-time on a real process. Someone must do the training. One very powerful approach is for a mid- or high-level manager to teach the first few times. Other possible methods include using a training department, a corporate process specialist, or outside consultant. Trainers can grasp the essentials of process mastering in a day's time. We can't overemphasize the value of management's commitment and continuing interest to the success of process mastering. It is essential! Our experience shows the training is most effective when done just in time, rather than "broadcasting" it to everyone. The learning starts to evaporate if it is not used immediately.

A pilot team is a good idea. You will need to get experience in leading a team and to work out the bugs in the supporting functions. No two organizations are exactly the same, so local needs must figure into your plans. The pilot group should work on a small process with likely success. By success, we mean the team will be able to agree on the "best known way" to complete the process master and for all to follow the standards. You will need a visible success to encourage others to join in willingly. The dragons can be slain by the more experienced groups to follow.

As you launch a process mastering effort and begin selecting processes to study, keep the following cautions in mind:

- Choose processes, team leaders, and teams carefully. You want successful outcomes.

- Don't overcommit and start too many teams at once. They take support, monitoring, and encouragement. You will learn as you gain experience.

- Remember that you start by standardizing and stabilizing processes, not reengineering them.

The discussion and planning that goes on with the person chosen to be team leader is very important. Some people refer to this as chartering the team. Haller refers to the "Contractual Phase" in his continuous improvement model. Accountability and responsibility must be clear to both parties.

The sponsor and team leader must define the preliminary boundaries of the process to be studied. One approach is to complete the following sentences:

1. The process starts with...

2. The process ends with...

3. The process includes...

4. The process excludes...

5. The connecting processes are....

It is helpful to actually sketch out a rough block diagram/flow chart of the major steps during the chartering phase.

A critical step in the discussion is for the sponsor to tell the team leader of anything that is off limits or that would be unacceptable to him/her. There is nothing much worse than to have a team do its best to master a process and have their work rejected by their sponsor.

Choosing Processes to Master

GENERAL CONSIDERATIONS

Another important decision that must be made is what process(es) to work on. Harrington makes the point that there are literally hundreds of business, as opposed to manufacturing, processes going on every day. "Over 80% of them are repetitive, things we do over and over again." There are various reasons for choosing certain processes. When you are beginning, it is important to choose processes that are under one department's or unit's control, that is, they don't cross department boundaries. The first few processes should be relatively small and simple so that the team learns how to do the mastering process and doesn't get bogged down in a very complicated business process. Once there is some initial success, some logical reasons for choosing one process over another are:

> "You should select a theme directly related to the customer or money."
>
> Shoji Shiba

- There is customer dissatisfaction

- There is too much variation

- There are high safety or environmental risks

- This process or series of processes are critical to key initiatives in using quality as a business strategy (Moen).

- The process crosses department boundaries, and there is need for better understanding and communication

- The process involves significant and repeating start-up and shut-down steps

- The process is done by people on several shifts, or it spans shifts.

PRIORITY

Process mastering is most effective when it is used to reach the organization's goals. The strategic planning process should be used to decide on key strategic objectives, key result areas, major improvement opportunities, and processes needing improvement. The planning process should be led by top management and is most effective when all levels of management are involved. Here is an example of the use of process mastering to help meet a strategic objective.

A key strategic objective may be: to define, target, and exploit the Southeast market through enhanced market intelligence and sales efforts.

A key result area might be: to develop products that provide price effectiveness or functional advantages for customers.

A major improvement opportunity could be: develop and introduce a mid-range Marvin Valve for the apartment and condominium market, by the end of the second quarter.

The only other Marvin Valve competitor has shoddy merchandise, but word on the street is that the Ajax Plumbing Parts company is going to enter the Marvin market with a good design.

The processes that may need to be mastered and improved could be: Valve Casting, Seat Machining, and customer service (Order Entry). The Valve Casting process has had a history of rough startups. When the Alban limiter was introduced, the first month's production ran more than 7 percent defects. When the process was mastered, the workers identified dozens of ways to reduce mold setup problems. After it had been through a process mastering cycle, the defect rate dropped to less than 0.2 percent. Because the new valve requires casting new alloys, the learning curve may be steep. The team can learn the tricks of the trade by inviting their raw material supplier to attend the process mastering meetings, and learning the best known casting methods directly from the metallurgist. The supplier is happy to work with the team, because it helps the supplier to completely understand and guide their customers' use of the alloys. The team understands most of the pitfalls before they start using the new materials.

The Seat Machining process had been a problem because the machines were not consistently set up for most efficiency. Some shifts ran 20 percent higher production, due to consistent calibration of the lathes. This inconsistency was eliminated by the team when process mastering was applied. All the shifts improved their setups. This enabled two workers to move into better jobs. By mastering the process again, the cycle will generate new suggestions for quality and reduction of rework. This waste reduction will allow for the use of less raw material and lower labor costs.

The Order Entry workers have had more turnover than usual, and the customer service level could be better, especially when entering new customer shipping directions. Several entry errors sent shipments to customers' headquarter addresses, rather than their production locations. For this reason alone, it is important to fix this process, because the other lines of products depend on the order entry people to get the most accurate data into the computer. Adding the new valve line will add to their workload, which could cause even more accuracy problems. Having a process master in place will allow the training of new workers in the shortest possible time. The retrieval and reshipping cost of one trailer load of valves would pay for all of the team's meeting costs.

The timing may be critical—the third quarter is the start of the construction season in the Southeast.

It will be critical to get into the market ahead of Ajax. Engineering should start designing prototypes while the Casting and Machining processes are mastered. The prototyping process is expected to take about two months. By the time the prototypes are approved, the Casting and Machining

> "...process control can be applied to any process that repeats and that can be measured; in other words, process control can be applied to a large number of diverse tasks. No matter what length the process cycle or how complex the task, process control can be applied to it."
>
> Shoji Shiba

processes will have been mastered, and be ready to start tooling up for the new valve production. The Order Entry team will start later, because adequate management support is critical, and two managers are focusing on the Casting and Machining team successes. When the first two teams are finished, the lessons learned can be applied to the Order Entry process master, which may shorten the mastering process. Another reason to start the Order Entry team later is to get the new Customer Service manager firmly settled in her job before adding team leadership responsibilities. The Order Entry team should be finished just about the time when the new valve brochures come back from the printer. The order entry process will be stabilized, and the new workers will understand the process, reducing entry errors and extra shipping costs. Within 12–16 weeks, all three teams should have stabilized their processes, saving productive time and cutting rework time. They will be ready for the rollout and extra work filling the pipeline with new valves.

BOUNDARIES AND SIZE

An important consideration is deciding where processes begin and end. The sustainability of the quality-improvement process hinges on individual team success and the resulting boost in morale. You will want to structure team charters to be sure the process mastering teams can complete their jobs in less than ten meetings. Six to eight meetings (6–8 hours) is the usual target.

How can you ensure the team finishes on time? The team's management sponsor and team leader define the process, including first and last steps to be mastered. There are two main ways this is commonly done. The first way is to look for natural breaks. The second is the time-honored seat-of-the-pants method.

Natural breaks are found when you walk (physically or mentally) through the process. Breaks occur where the nature of the work changes, where barriers have been put in place, or where departments begin and end. "Barriers" means physical or mental walls, which separate functions. The old reliable seat-of-the-pants method uses an educated guess to set process boundaries. The best rule of thumb we've found is this one: the process should have six to nine major steps. If more than nine major steps are found, you should consider dividing the process master.

As mentioned above, the right size processes to be mastered usually contain six to nine major steps. A major step is one that is indispensable to the process. It may contain up to five substeps. An example is helpful to visualize a major step. A common process is "Issuing payroll checks." An example of a major step would be "Compute hours worked." Substeps would be Collect time cards, Add time columns, and Verify employee math.

Some examples of the right-size processes we have seen mastered include these:

Check safety equipment before starting the day

Fill products into bottles

Close bottles of product

Purchase raw materials

Change gas-chromatograph columns

Plate microbiological samples

Inspect truckloads for cleanliness

Fill an order

Pay invoices

Load a truck

Take an order

Service a fire extinguisher

Tune an engine

Wax a floor

Assemble ingredients

Make a batch

Clean dust collectors

Count inventory

Schedule production

Log sample requests

Pack overseas shipments

Standardize a pH meter

Run a taste panel

Clean a ribbon blender

Receive truckloads of alcohol.

Other processes that could be the right size include:

Register a patient

Clean a motel room

Set up a bank account

Route a delivery

Do a dental checkup

Close the books

Design a marketing plan

Communicate a price increase

Do a credit check

Set up a training room

Qualify a prospect

Inspect a bridge

Schedule a seminar

Maintain a mailing list

Set up a computer

Investigate a crime scene

Fuel a plane

Close a contract

Prepare fast food

Drill a well

Prep a new car

Purchase shares of stock

Pour a concrete floor

Collect a slow debt

Recharge an air conditioner

Operate a coordinate measuring machine

Schedule a concert

Calibrate a lathe

Complete a tax audit

Make a sales call.

A too-large process will delay the schedule of standardization and improvements. It will also demoralize team members. The effect will be to slow down the process mastering momentum. A process that is the right size will energize team members. The momentum will build for continuing standardization and improvement within the organization. A process that is too small and trivial will be a waste of time.

Imagine you are the manager of a city's water system. The entire system would be too large to master at once. Mastering the 30-second orthotolidine test for chlorine would be trivial. An appropriate process to be mastered would be billing customers.

Coordination of Effort

A strong case can be made for centralized direction and control of the process mastering effort—to what extent will have to be determined by each organization. There are numerous reasons this is so. First of all, centralization fosters uniformity, less variation. The quality of training can be maintained. Activity can be directed. When the processes to be mastered are decided based on corporate initiatives, there is a need to see that the most critical processes to the success of the initiatives are worked on first. This, as well as simply monitoring activity in general, can be done best from a centralized perspective.

When processes become fairly large and particularly when they cross functional boundaries, there is the need for coordination and communication. This role can be carried out by the person or office at the center of the effort. This is especially important when "territory" becomes an issue. The central office can remain neutral and help the parties involved to see the greater good of working together.

Another very important reason to centralize control is to improve efficiency. It isn't uncommon for several departments to have similar processes. It is only logical to take what was done in one department, and use it or modify it for another department. A few examples of this idea are: pre-trip inspections of trucks or forklifts, monthly fire extinguisher or ladder inspections, safe docking of trucks at a warehouse shipping dock, and customer order taking.

"People support what they create."

Margaret Wheatley

When there is a central registry, there is an opportunity to establish a tickler file to regularly follow up to see if the process masters are being used, replaced, or modified. This resulting communication and data base allow for centralized accounting of effort and employee involvement. It also provides the organization with a way to monitor and measure accomplishment.

Support

Clearly the most important item of support is the manager's continuing interest in the process mastering effort. This translates into physical involvement as much as possible, at least as the effort is getting started. This interest also translates into expectations of lower level managers and supervisors. They need to understand and "enroll" in the value of doing process masters. Chances of this occurring will improve if everyone has been involved in creating the aim of the organization and if they have participated in or at least understand why work on certain processes will further the success of the organization. Management must be certain to remove structural impediments and to send clear signals about its priorities. That is, it can't lead the process mastering parade with a banner exclaiming how important it is, and then when things get a little tense, put production or some other issue ahead of time for process mastering, so that month-end statements can look better. This would be a sure sign that management speaks with a forked tongue.

"Developing good habits. Building processes into everyone's work to maintain the gains. (It's easy to make things clean and organized once—the key is to keep it that way.)"

Seiketsu

Management must see to it that all employees receive necessary training. Of course the involved employees require training in process mastering. They also need training in working as a team. In particular, they need to know how to make decisions and how to work together. Learning how to work cooperatively in a team should not be underestimated. It is not easy, and it is vital for success. We know of no better resource to help with this matter than *The Team Handbook* referenced earlier. The team also needs training in flowcharts and flowcharting. *Mapping Work Processes,* by Dianne Galloway; or *The Basics of Process Mapping,* by Robert Damelio, may be helpful. Some, if not all, employees will need leadership and group facilitation skills. Generally, we don't feel it is necessary to have a person fill the role of facilitator in process mastering teams. If, however, a team gets stuck or is just not being efficient or successful, it is helpful to have a trained facilitator meet with the team leader prior to and following a meeting and to observe the team meeting. With this assistance, most teams get back on the track.

The most precious item of support that must be made available is the time of the employees. Rarely do organizations have people with extra time. On the other hand, the average of one or two hours a week invested in process improvement is rarely missed—even in the short term. Our observation is that the change of pace, the learning, the stimulation alone offset the production time lost. It should be noted that overtime may be required. This could occur when there just isn't any other time to get people together, or it could occur when it is necessary to get people from two shifts to the same meetings.

To be effective, teams must be provided with some space to meet. It doesn't need to be elaborate or fancy. In fact, it is best if it is near the process being mastered, reasonably quiet, and equipped with a flip chart, pens, sticky notes, and perhaps an erasable board.

Management should also provide some staff support. Teams often need someone efficient with the use of computer word processing and flowchart software programs. Also, on occasion, it will be necessary for a team to have access to experts or specialists. This will need to be arranged and supported.

INTERNETWORKING OF PROCESS MASTERS

In managing and communicating process masters, you can take advantage of recent advances in information technology (IT). Off-the-shelf Internet-standards-based software offers acceptable reliability, scalability, and interoperability to be used as the basis for implementing process mastering across any organization. However, the great flexibility of these tools increases the importance of up-front planning.

According to Horch, the technical aspects of creating and disseminating process masters is becoming a relatively straightforward matter of selecting a solution based on open Internet standards (such as e-mail, newsgroups, Web browsers, and servers). Computer networks based on Internet standards are now recognized as the most cost-effective approach throughout all levels of an organization. Building on Internet standards also gives great flexibility in selecting vendors and software packages, since any Internet standard by definition is designed to work with a large number of other systems.

Several buzzwords may be useful to know. The "Internet" is a public network of networks, designed primarily to connect one network with another. So, if you are putting information out to the public using any standard protocol such as a web server or e-mail, you are using the Internet. An "intranet" is a network based on the same standard protocols, but within a single organization. So, if you are putting information on a web server inside the company so marketing can see what manufacturing is doing, you are using an intranet. Finally, an "extranet" is using the same standard protocols to communicate to a defined group of people outside of an organization. So, if you are putting information on a password-protected web site for your suppliers but not necessarily the whole world to see, you are using an extranet.

In many respects, the technical solution may be the least difficult aspect of implementing process masters across an enterprise. Assuming a ubiquitous information infrastructure (in the sense that everyone or each unit in an organization has access to a computer on an enterprise-wide network), then in a very real sense the new tools allow anyone to share information with anyone else in the organization. And when the corporate network is connected to the Internet, extending to other corporate and public networks, then everyone in the world is essentially connected.

Although in practice this situation is not completely realized, a staggering amount of information can be made available by the types of networks that companies are now putting into place and hooking up to the Internet. You should assume that the information technology at your disposal will allow anyone in the organization to create and maintain information that can be shared with any other individuals or groups inside or outside of the organization. The business planning challenge is to identify and manage the who, what, where, when, why, and how of information flow in the organization.

Like any other bit of corporate data, process masters have an information life cycle, which can be broken down into four phases: creation, distribution, maintenance, and destruction.

The business management decisions that must be made as new process masters are created include what format will be used, who will be responsible for putting them on line, and who will have access.

The distribution phase is the most crucial, because this typically affects the most people, and is the reason for the information's existence. There are two main approaches to distribution: "push" and "pull." In "push," the recipients don't have to do anything (although they may need to tune in to whatever is being pushed their way). The distributor selects who will receive the information and sends it to them. "Push" can be anything from e-mail to video broadcasting.

With "pull," on the other hand, the recipients have to actively select and retrieve the information. Bulletin boards and web sites are pull systems: nothing gets distributed unless the recipient actively seeks it out. An index, or even several different indices, direct recipients to the appropriate information. A search engine is an essential part of a good pull system for large amounts of information.

Push or pull, the access control to the information system needs to be established. Who should have access to which kinds of information? Even if the goal is to have everyone participate in process mastering, people should not spend too much time and energy on the new information resources at the expense of doing the rest of their jobs. The process master distribution system must be planned to fit well with other business processes and the organization's culture.

Updates also need to be handled intelligently. One of the major advantages of adopting the latest information technology is the idea of "living documents" that are continually improved over time. As with the distribution system, care must be taken that the process of updating information does not get out of hand. A business decision must be made as to who will have authority and responsibility to make updates. A version control system should be instituted for tracking changes made by different people and for providing the ability to "roll back" to any previous versions.

Finally, the destruction of old information should not be overlooked. A plan should be developed for retracting process masters from distribution, and either archiving them for a certain period or destroying them.

As this section indicates, the technology applicable to maintaining and communicating process masters has made great strides recently. It is still advancing rapidly. But like any business process, fancy technology cannot replace good planning! Management should be reminded that the two main reasons that you would want to internetwork your process master effort are to allow easy updating and easy communicating to others doing the same process or developing similar process masters.

The reader should not become concerned about the need for computers, software, erasable boards, etc. These items only help with the presentation. You can do process mastering quite well with a pencil and paper.

Overall, process mastering requires only a small investment. As mentioned above, the most important investment is basically free, management's interest and support.

Recognition

Managers often feel it is necessary to recognize teams for completing process masters. Recognition for work done will vary from organization to organization depending on their cultures. Based on recent research by Edward Deci and reviews of social psychology research by Alfie Kohn, the best recognition, or if you take it even further, the best reward for work done, is intrinsic. It's the feeling you get when you have had a chance to collaborate with other people, you have challenging work to do, and you have some choice in how the work is done. So in the case of recognition, reward, and celebration, we believe that less is better. However, this does not mean that the work and accomplishments should not be communicated to peers and higher management. This communication is vital for a number of reasons. Management needs to know what is going on in the organization's continuous improvement efforts. The workers need to know that management approves and supports their efforts. They also need feedback and encouragement to continue. Customers, suppliers, and other process workers need to know of the completion of process masters, because upstream and downstream processes will be directly affected by reduced variation. Excitement is often generated when processes improve in adjacent work areas.

References

Damelio, R. (1996). *The Basics of Process Mapping.* New York: Quality Resources.

Deci, E. L. (1996). *Why We Do What We Do.* New York: Penguin Press.

Galloway, D. (1994). *Mapping Work Processes.* Milwaukee: Quality Press.

Haller, H. S. (1993). *Empowerment Operationalized* Monograph. Cleveland: Harold S. Haller & Company, pp. 8–14.

Harrington, H. J. (1991). *Business Process Improvement: The Breakthrough Strategy for Total Quality, Productivity, and Competitiveness.* New York: McGraw-Hill, pp. 10, 17–18.

Horch, F. W. Trinet Services, Inc., 150 Fayettville Street Mall, Suite 1340, Raleigh, NC 27601. Private conversation.

Imai, M. (1996). *Kaizen; The Key to Japan's Competitive Success.* Toronto: Random House.

Kane, E. J. (1992). "Process Management Methodology Brings Uniformity to DBS." *Quality Progress.* June, p. 42.

Kohn, A. (1993). *Punished By Rewards: The Trouble With Gold Stars, Incentive Plans, A's, Praise and Other Bribes.* New York: Houghton Mifflin.

Moen, R. (1993). *Quality As a Business Strategy.* Associates in Process Improvement, Austin, p. 11.

Rummler, G. A. and A. P. Brache (1990). *Improving Performance: How to Manage the White Space on the Organization Chart.* San Francisco: Jossey-Bass.

Seiketsu (1991). *The 5S's: Five Keys to a Total Quality Environment by Takashi Osada.* Tokyo: Asian Productivity Organization.

Shiba, S. (1993). *A New American TQM.* Portland: Productivity Press, pp. 59, 83.

Wheatley, M. (1995). *Self-Organizing Systems: Creating the Capacity for Continuous Change.* Quality Satellite Network, Inc.

Chapter 4

TRICKS, TRAPS, AND ALLIGATORS

Below is a list of some general observations and experiences that we have seen in our process mastering experience. It is hoped that by sharing them, we will help prepare the reader for some otherwise unexpected encounters. The authors look forward to hearing of other Tricks, Traps, and Alligators that you, as process mastering practitioners, run into.

> "A general maxim in quality control for engineering or marketing is standardize routine tasks and avoid routine defects, so that you can focus on being creative."
>
> Shoji Shiba

Individual Freedom and Creativity

Americans think of themselves as creative and individualistic. They want to do things "my way." People feel that if a task is standardized, it is boring. Kouzes and Posner talk about "The Paradox of Routines" by pointing out that leaders must challenge standard processes or routines because they can stifle creativity and get you into a rut. On the other hand, routines are essential to having "a definable, consistent, measurable, and efficient operation." So, it is very important to consider the tradeoff between need and value of standardization to reduce variation and the feeling that the person doing the task has no choice. Brian Joiner devotes an entire chapter of *Fourth Generation Management* to this subject as it relates to quality improvement. He acknowledges the resistance people normally exhibit toward standardization, and he points out the superior results that occur when teams "develop and adhere to best-known methods." He suggests that where standardization has been most successful the companies typically:

- create standards judiciously

- involve many people

- begin with "check" of the standardize, do, check, act cycle

- build an organizational memory

- train and retrain.

We believe process mastering as presented in this book supports Joiner's five points about successful standardization. It is not important to standardize steps that don't introduce safety hazards or variation to the output. That is, they can be done any old way without affecting the next customer.

> "Having standardized, low-waste processes does not mean that our work places have to become dull and lifeless. The new challenge is to create a new excitement, one that is based on rapid improvement and delighted customers—not one that is based on heroic brute-force efforts."
>
> Brian L. Joiner

The OSHA Paper Trail

When the OSHA inspector arrives, the training records may be out of date or incomplete. To avoid a citation, safety training processes must be documented, including training dates and content. Process mastering meetings often include safety personnel, especially when safety hazards are present in the process. Employees may have difficulty explaining the safe operation of the Framois Cutter, but if a current process master is posted in the work area, chances are better that the worker will be: a) working safely, and b) able to explain the safety precautions.

The Guide Who Deserts the Client

A manager with extremely good intentions set up some teams for processes in his sales area. He found participation to be excruciatingly tedious. Because of his lack of patience, the teams languished and died. The leader needs to understand that chartering a team means following through to the end.

Agree on the Words

The team members should make sure they agree on the exact wording in the process master documents during their meetings. In other words, it is not good to leave the exact wording up to one individual who may be responsible for taking notes or to communicate to a typist. This can lead to misunderstanding and rework.

On the other hand, team leaders and team members must be sensitive to the fact that some people get totally frustrated and demoralized when they think wordsmithing has gotten out of hand. This situation must be accommodated.

Schedule for Meetings Matters

It is strongly suggested that team meetings be scheduled on a regular basis, that is, the same time and the same day of the week until the master is done. This helps people plan and avoids the discontinuity and loss of efficiency that occurs if weeks are missed.

Length of Meetings Can Vary

It is certainly possible to do a process master in one sitting. Although this isn't recommended, it may be necessary or desirable if the members of the team come from scattered locations. A further modification may be to meet for two or three hours at a time when the team members are not from the immediate nearby work group.

Wide Area Process Master Development

Process masters can be developed over long distances. This opportunity could arise when similar processes are done at several locations. In this case, one or two people at one location can initiate a process master. Their materials can be mailed, faxed, or e-mailed to other locations for consideration and revision. Through subsequent mailings and telephone conversations, the final process master can be developed.

Process Mastering as a Diagnostic Tool

Process masters can work for brand new processes or where the "process" is hard to distinguish, that is, where there is a mess that doesn't seem to have an owner or defined boundaries. Getting interested parties in the same room and using the disciplined process master approach can help clean up former problem areas.

A Second Chance at Process Improvement

Many companies have experienced process improvement start-up headaches and regrouped to try it again. False starts seem to center around mega-team improvement projects. Many have started down that path and found roadblocks around the second corner. Many teams were doomed from the start. Processes were unstable, not well understood, and not accurately written down. The teams were shooting at moving targets. Processes that are not standardized can be changed, but not permanently improved. Standardized processes provide a stable launch pad for an improvement effort.

Sponsor Sets Boundaries

Sponsors must bear the responsibility for making clear to the team any limits or unacceptable steps in a process. Ideally, this should be done when the team is chartered. This avoids the awkwardness, rework, and possible demoralization that can occur if something unacceptable comes up during final signoff by the sponsor. The sponsor is advised to interpret "unacceptable" only when it truly is!

Monster Process

Occasionally, even after initial, careful planning by the sponsor and team leader, the size of a process gets out of hand. This becomes apparent when the team can't settle on six to nine major steps in the flowchart, or there are far more than five substeps under one or more major steps, or there are many decision steps that cause the process to get very complicated. When this happens, a decision has to be made whether to continue developing a large, complicated master or to break it into several smaller, simpler masters.

The situation should dictate the decision. Here are a few thoughts to consider: Does the team have the knowledge, stamina, and support to complete the large master? Will the completed large master help in communicating to others the complexity of the process and, therefore, help the overall organization's effort, or will it detract or complicate understanding? Is there a small but vital "subprocess" that is most critical to the overall effort? Can it be simply broken into small processes that when connected can be managed as a system? Does it cross department boundaries?

Be advised that dealing with a monster process is not an uncommon occurrence, especially with people with little experience in process mastering. Be patient and work through it, keeping everyone informed as you do. Remember, there is no right or wrong decision; however, when in doubt, go small.

When an Impasse Is Reached

Sometimes, even with thorough planning, training, and best intentions, a team will hit a barrier. It

". . .most groups inevitably step into the 'should be' before analyzing the 'what is'."

Dianne Galloway

could be that the group cannot agree on the best way to do something or, heaven forbid, the team sponsor can't accept something about the completed master. There are several things that can be done. The team can run experiments, gather data, and decide what is the best way. An outside expert, impartial observer, or facilitator could be brought in to make a recommendation and/or help the group through the impasse. Or, if all else fails, the process master team can be put in neutral for a while. This gives time for emotions to cool and things to be put in perspective. Generally, weeks or months later, the effort can be revived and completed with little effort. And finally, although we've never seen it, it might be possible for a process master to be completed and have a team member be a dissenter at sign-off time.

Get Everyone Talking

We have seen some team members who sat on the sidelines and "passed" when asked to join the discussion. Or, a vocal member drowned out opposition. The team leader needs to balance time constraints with the need for complete participation. Consensus requires that everyone be encouraged to speak freely.

Failure by Success

When starting process mastering, it is new, exciting, and challenging. People enjoy being listened to and working as a team. They get a taste of what it can be like to make things better. At this point, various things can happen, and one of them might be called failure by success. When a group of people complete a process master and grasps what the potential improvements might be for the process, they take off making improvements. At that point, the process mastering routine seems like plodding along or an anchor that holds them back. It could feel like an unnecessary bureaucracy.

There is no easy solution for this, short of dictating that the process masters must be kept current. It helps to turn the process master into an "on-line" document where it can be changed on the go with ease. Some companies use blackboards at the jobsite to change standards "on the fly."

Worker-Manager Teams

We have never encountered a situation where workers weren't eager to study and help improve work processes. They know best the frustrations associated with trying to get the job done and satisfying the customer. Occasionally, when workers are part of a labor union, there is uncertainty about the objective or about the decision structure when a process mastering effort is begun. And this situation should not be taken lightly.

In 1993, the United States National Labor Relations Board voted unanimously that several safety and fitness committees of one company were illegal "labor organizations" under the National Labor Relations Act of 1935. These committees had to be disbanded. We do not believe this ruling applies to process mastering teams as suggested in this book. It only makes sense, however, to give consideration to the misunderstanding that can result if all parties are not informed. In organizations where unions exist, it is imperative for the company and union to agree in advance on issues relating to process mastering teams.

Worker Apprehension

If the culture is not right, if the workers do not feel secure, they may be reluctant to participate in writing down all the details about how they do a process. They fear that once the processes that they work in are fully defined, they could be replaced by workers with less experience or skill or workers at a lower pay scale. They may also fear that the process measurements will be used to evaluate them and not the process capability. These are natural feelings and should be expected to a greater or lesser degree in each situation.

This is a golden opportunity for management to drive out these fears. A policy should be stated before any teams begin that no employee will suffer because of a team effort. As processes are mastered and no one loses his/her job and when management concentrates on measuring the process and not the people, a new relationship or culture can be born.

Draw It

Drawings, sketches, or photos are powerful tools in communicating the "best known ways" on the key step worksheet. Often, a team member has a talent for drawing. The team member's input helps gain team ownership, so we encourage you to use this hidden talent to create illustrations of key process steps. It is easiest to draw the diagram on $8\frac{1}{2}$ x 11 paper and reduce it on the copier. The copy comes out better than the original.

Don't Overdo It

It is most productive to standardize only the critical process steps. The people who do the work decide which steps must be done only one way. Safety specialists may help the team decide where safety is an issue. Safety hazards are always standardized to help keep the employees safe.

It is a waste of time to let the team come to consensus about steps that make no difference. They have better things to do.

Employee Ownership

Employees should be allowed to feel that they share ownership of the process masters. If they see that they have some input on their jobs, they will be much more likely to follow the standards. This is a result of intrinsic motivation. If the team members see no reason to standardize a step, it will be difficult to get them to follow the standard. We have seen nearly all process employees follow the process master, even if they were only peripherally involved in its development. On the other hand, consider the number of SOPs written each year by managers or engineers that are not followed or updated.

Extrinsic forms of "motivation" will not get employees to follow SOPs or process masters if the document is not accurate. The actual process will drift toward the operator's personal comfort, rather than toward customer satisfaction.

Avoid Data Paralysis

Some teams gather data and never put it to use. After you have developed a process master and identified parameters to be measured, it is critical that the data be used to improve the process. We suggest that you gather data on a critical process parameter for 20–25 occurrences and plot the data on a graph. After analyzing the data, *do something* if warranted. Don't get trapped into gathering data because it is "the thing to do." Gather data to learn something, to make improvements.

> "The only reason for collecting data is to take action."
>
> William W.
> Sherkenbach

Doing It Without Benefit of Expert Help

A few managers have heard the process mastering overview and tried to lead teams without proper training. The results resembled a train wreck. Teams wasted months. Leadership came out of it confused and disillusioned. Workers blamed management for another "flavor of the month." The long-term damage included virtual stoppage of the continual improvement effort.

References

Galloway, D. (1994). *Mapping Work Processes*. Milwaukee: Quality Press, p. vii.

Joiner, B. L. (1994). *Fourth Generation Management: The New Business Consciousness*. New York: McGraw-Hill, pp. 187, 220.

Kouzes, J. M., Posner, B. Z. (1987). *The Leadership Challenge*. San Francisco: Jossey-Bass, pp. 47, 48.

Sherkenbach, W. W. (1995). *Constancy of Purpose Process Workbook*.

Shiba, S. (1993). *A New American TQM*. Portland, OR: Productivity Press.

Chapter 5

STORIES, MEASUREMENTS, AND EXAMPLES

Walk the Talk

Employees do not need much encouragement to get their help in process improvement. We have observed that the line workers are much more ready to accept change than middle managers are. There are a couple of prerequisites to their acceptance of change, however.

One need is for the employees to feel they are a part of the change process. Another important need that must be covered early is their own security. There must be a clear, unequivocal signal from the highest level of management that their job is not in danger due to gains in efficiency. A nationwide food company (call it Integral Ingredients) rolled out a total quality improvement process to every plant location, explaining that the employees would be even more secure if the company was more prosperous. One of the first applications of process standardization was the roller-drying of a food-starch-based, natural protein product. Integral Ingredients had two roller-dryers, each with a packaging line and palletizing crew.

A major improvement in productivity allowed one entire line to be turned off. This meant that 6 people now could do what 12 people had done the week before. Because of the Board of Director's policy that employees would not suffer because of an increase in productivity, those employees were transferred into other parts of the plant at the same or higher rates of pay.

This story was told at each new TQI rollout by one of the affected employees, who transferred into the maintenance department. Because of this early decision and the support of management, this story spread throughout the 17 locations of the company, building trust and allowing a successful implementation of the TQI philosophy. This level of commitment by management is critical to getting employees involved in the improvement of their own processes.

One of the later rollouts was done in a Midwestern plant. A critical process for delivery of the product was spray-drying. A normal part of the daily operation was to stop drying occasionally to brush the starch off the inside walls of the tower. This step was troublesome because of the machine downtime, and because foreign materials could get into the product while the doors were open. The supervisor wanted to standardize the cleanup process, in order to gain as much productivity as possible.

In the discussion, the question was asked, "Why does starch accumulate on the walls in the first place?" The question was captured on the parking lot list and the process standardized with the best known way to brush down the dryer. Later, the team was asked to find out why starch sticks and how to reduce the problem. The team members tried several suggestions before they found the best combination of air flow, temperature, and percent water in the slurry, which resulted in little starch accumulating on the dryer walls. The improvement amounted to the labor of two employees per shift, six employees total. One employee transferred into scheduling, one into maintenance, one into shipping. The other three moved into downstream packaging. Those employees never would have reported the productivity improvement if they had not been confident of their future employment.

Unnecessary Work and Expense

Sometimes as process masters are developed, some surprising things are learned. Such was the case when three managers from three petroleum terminals were working together to put together a process master to standardize the receipt of a tank truckload of alcohol.

The process mastering meeting was going along fine until they began discussing the best known way to sample the alcohol in the tank.

The first manager said he took a graduated cylinder, climbed up on top of the transport trailer, opened the hatch, and dipped the graduated cylinder into the alcohol. He then carefully climbed down, after closing the hatch, and placed the hydrometer in the cylinder and took a reading.

The second manager said he found that routine too dangerous and had installed a spigot in the line leading from the transport to the storage tank. So, as the product was being pumped into the tank, he filled his graduated cylinder from the spigot— on the ground.

The third manager had a procedure like the second manager except that he rinsed the cylinder out one time before filling it with the official test sample.

Upon hearing these three approaches, the facilitator for this session asked two questions.

1. What is the correct hydrometer reading?

2. What will you do if you get an unacceptable reading and the product is already being pumped into the large storage tank, thus contaminating already received good product? The questions prompted everyone to realize that no one knew what the correct/acceptable hydrometer reading should be. This realization prompted another question.

3. What do you do with the reading you take? One manager said he sent the number along with a lot of other load data to the refinery. Two managers said they did that also, but in addition, they sent a copy to the pipeline pump station office. The facilitator, having heard that, suggested that the team call the refinery and the pipeline office to research these questions.

The pipeline office said, "We don't know why you keep sending that report to us; we never use it." The refinery office said,

"We don't know why you send that to us; we only need three pieces of information and specific gravity of the alcohol is not one of them."

So, for over ten years, through all kinds of weather, employees were putting themselves at risk to take samples of very flammable alcohol for no reason. For over ten years there was a waste of personnel time to write, transmit, and handle data that was never used.

Upon having this experience, these three managers were eager to look into other processes under their control.

The Effect of Arbitrary Numerical Goals

During the development of a process master in a laboratory, the team reached a point where they were discussing how many times a cellulose thimble should be used before replacement. The thimbles are used in a test that extracts fat from animal feeds. The standard wisdom and recommendations from the supplier suggested the lightweight thimbles could be reused two or three times. Sensing an opportunity to save some money, the lab manager suggested to the lead chemist that she try the more expensive and heavier weight thimbles, and to try to make them last for ten cycles. After doing some experimentation, she found the thimbles could last for ten cycles before being thrown away, so the new disposal cycle was implemented. Upon hearing this, the facilitator, at the next team meeting, asked why the number ten was arbitrarily chosen. After a bit of embarrassment, everyone realized there was no good reason other than it was so much better than two or three, and it would result in a certain monetary savings.

Subsequently, further research was done, and the team found that the thimbles lasted much longer. In fact, with the use of control charts, they can now determine when to change thimbles. On average, they can be used 35 times.

In financial terms, this team went from using a lightweight thimble costing $1.95 each and used it two or three times, to a heavy weight thimble costing $2.72 each and used 35 times. That means going from $.65/use to $.08/use—a savings of $.57 per use. At the time of this writing, the lab analyzed an average of 21 samples for fat each day. This resulted in a savings of over $3,000 per year. The bottom line for this lab team was "master your processes and don't set arbitrary numerical goals."

As a footnote, the thimble supplier was so pleased that the team shared their results with him, that he took back all the stock of lightweight thimbles without a restocking charge.

Partnering With Customers Pays Off

An Indiana shipping department cut truckloading time by 30 percent when the order-runners developed and used standard pallet-marking methods, as a result of a process master done with the warehouse crew and the customer. Their Florida customer's receiving time was reduced by 20 hours per week because of the same shipping department's uniform stacking and marking of pallets.

Employees Improve Sample Turnaround Time

In an Indianapolis food plant, the quality control employees cut moisture testing turnaround time. The turnaround time for sample logging, testing, and approval delayed delivery of fresh products to external customers. The technicians mastered the sample routing process and then identified several unnecessary delays. When they mastered the process in February 1992, more than 22 percent of the moisture tests took more than four hours. By June 1992, the process had been streamlined, and only 2 percent of the moisture tests took more than four hours.

Packaging Employees Cut Bag and Labor Waste

The White Premix department in an Indiana plant had struggled for years to fill and seal two-pound polyethylene bags of a fluffy candy powder. The bags appeared to be sealed perfectly, but a bag or two in every hundred popped open when the product was shipped on trucks. When the bags arrived at the customer's dock, the customer had to sort out the leakers and wipe the powder off the outside of the other bags. This caused lots of headaches for the customer, and they passed the sorting costs back to the powder department.

The end came when the customer threatened to buy from a competitor. In order to keep the customer, the employees mastered the premix department maintenance processes. The mastering team learned that heating wires wore through the Teflon sealing pads and could then cut through the plastic bags. By replacing the pads every week, the leaking bags were nearly eliminated. A six-meeting investment resulted in a 99 percent reduction in leaking packages and eliminated the customer's sorting of packages.

Standard Test Methods Required

In order to monitor the pulp strength of the raw material for newsprint made in high-speed paper machines, a Canadian process team developed a new wet strength test procedure. The team instructed each of the five lab technicians to run the tests.

Everyone was disappointed when the new test method produced erratic results. They thought they had a complete and straightforward procedure for testing the pulp, but the results varied widely between the technicians who ran the tests—even though all the technicians were given the same instructions and were equally capable.

So the process team assembled all the technicians and began asking questions. They started through the flowchart steps and came to the step of thawing the frozen sample. Originally the process team did not consider sample thawing to be a key step. However since things were not going well, all their previous ideas had to be re-examined.

The meeting facilitator asked each technician in turn how they thawed the sample. To everyone's surprise, including their manager, one technician boiled the sample in water, two thawed the sample in a microwave oven, one thawed the sample in the hot air oven, and one technician let the sample sit out on the counter overnight. As a result of these different methods of thawing samples, some pulp was poached, some pulp was cooked from the inside out, some pulp was baked from the outside in, and some pulp started to decompose as it thawed.

At this point, the team, including the technicians, decided on the best known way to thaw the samples, and the technicians agreed to follow the standard.

Within a few days, the variation in the test results disappeared. They could predict wet strength and run the newsprint more smoothly, with less waste. The process knowledge of the hands-on staff was the key to successful improvement.

Contributed by Dr. Harold S. Huller.

Measurements of Process Health

As mentioned in Chapter 2, for whatever reason, many teams have difficulty finding or choosing measurements for their processes. Many times this is simply because there is no apparent or obvious thing to measure. Many times the major concern is that the process develops data very slowly—over a long period of time. Occasionally, measurement ideas come slowly because people are afraid of how the data will be used. Will it be used to criticize? Will the messenger be killed? For these and other reasons, we have decided to give some specific suggestions for measurements.

REASONS TO MEASURE

There are a number of reasons to make measurements. They are important to determine the gap between what a process is presently capable of and what the desire for the process is. A set of measurements can be used as a baseline to just know where you are. Measurements allow you to compare your process to some other process. Measurements appropriately displayed can be a powerful tool for communicating vital information that can be used to inform and persuade. Measurements of system parameters can also tell if a process is stable or if it is unpredictable. Seeking measurements elicits ingenuity from people about what can be measured, how

> "The productivity and effectiveness of any function can be measured by some combination of cost, time, quality, quantity, or human reaction indices."
>
> Jac. Fitz-enz

to measure it, and what the measurements mean. Measurements focus attention on important issues. Requests for measurements signal a genuine interest in what is going on and clarify expectations. Measurements provide the data to make intelligent decisions.

CLUES TO FIND MEASUREMENT OPPORTUNITIES

> "There is no substitute for getting out in the workplace to collect data. People who have tried to collect data have a greater appreciation for what their processes are capable of doing and what kinds of data they are likely to encounter. This experience makes them just more likely to understand how the tools can help them put their data to good use."
>
> Lynda Finn with Sue Reynard and Casey Garhart

There are numerous places to look for measurement opportunities. Measure what the process set out to accomplish. Look at what others measure. Look for what is important to the customer. This suggests that the customer should be asked. Look for decision points in the process. Look for feedback loops in the process. Look for places where errors or rework routinely occur. Look for areas that might generate data that would help communicate to others. Measurements of system parameters over time can also tell if a process is stable or if it is unpredictable. Describe and observe what the process does, and many times this can give some ideas of possible measurements.

Measurement Suggestions

Appendix C contains a random list of measures that could be considered when a process mastering team is unable to find a suitable measure for a process. The hope is that the items listed will trigger a creative measurement idea.

When having difficulty finding a measurement for something like management, describe what processes the managers do. Then many observable acts can lead to meaningful measurements.

More Measurement Hints

The power of measurements should not be underestimated. As the sayings go, what gets measured gets managed and what gets measured gets done. This should not be taken lightly because if the wrong thing(s) get(s) measured, bad things can happen. Goldratt indicates that many times measurements are inextricably linked to policies that can become the constraint to a system. Sometimes

A family of measures typically incorporates the following types of measures:

productivity
cycle time
quality
resource utilization costs
timeliness

these measurements/policies are buried way down in an organization, and no one understands the damage they do.

There are two areas of measurements, output or outcome and task. Output or outcome measurements can be used to measure what the process achieved. They can be used to monitor the ongoing health of the process. Is it stable? Is it meeting customers' expectations? These measures are like an ongoing report card. Task measurements are used to measure upstream before a lot of effort or material is invested. This is before work becomes irreversible or major resources are committed. This can be where mistakes have been made in the past, where safety or timing is critical, or where work is handed from one person to another. The two areas of measurements should be acknowledged as being distinct and used accordingly.

It is important to establish and agree on who, what, where, how, and when to take a measurement. This sounds simple, but experience suggests otherwise. The method and frequency of the measurements must be determined and monitored. Taking data measurements is often viewed as extra work and not part of getting the work out. Therefore, even with the best intentions, data gathering, if it is not reinforced, trails off and is soon forgotten.

Dickenson suggests, if data-gathering-trail-off, personnel turnover, or measurement management are a problem, then a measures' computer database should be considered. The key elements in such a database are:

- Raw data
- Code name or number for the measure
- Date established and last updated
- Owner's name, telephone number, etc.
- Measure's name and operational definition (method of measurement, frequency, and criteria for success— higher-the-better, lower-the-better, or target-the-best).

When measurements are gathered in such a database and made available on request or published periodically, a number of things can occur. Teams can get ideas for appropriate measures. What teams are measuring can be communicated and appreciated. Regular data gathering can be monitored.

At AT&T Bell Laboratories, they say: "The effectiveness of a measure of quality can be evaluated by the degree to which it is:

- related to customer requirements
- practical to implement
- easy to understand
- able to drive desired behavior
- developed with input from consensus with work groups
- specific."

Examples of Process Masters

What follows are two actual examples of process masters. Only the names of the participants have been changed. As you review them, you may wonder why certain decisions were made, why certain words were chosen, etc. All we can say is that at the point in time that the teams did these process masters, their words best described the processes.

As you begin generating process masters, you may find a different format works better for your organization. You should feel free to adjust. But you should establish uniformity within your organization.

Process Master

for

Promotional Support Material
Inventory Management
From Time of Ordering of Material to
Shipment to Members or Departments

Process Master #37

Date: March 18, 1996

Our process master team has identified and written down the best known ways to carry out our process. By signing below, I agree to follow the attached process master whenever possible. I understand that exceptional situations may force a temporary change in the process. When this happens, I will act in the best interests of my customers. I will also turn in a Process Master Exception Report of the temporary changes for possible updating of the process master.

Team Sponsor:	Lynn Headings
Team Leader:	Jim Welsh
Process Team Members:	Shirley Stauffer
	Jay Krouse
	Ron Hoch
	Larry Girvin

Dates of Revisions:

Group Norms

1. Be on time for meetings

2. Be honest

3. No put-downs

4. Be open and frank

5. Give high priority to this assignment

6. Agree to abide by what we decide

7. Be sensitive to everybody's issues and interests

Figure 29

External Customer "A" Chart

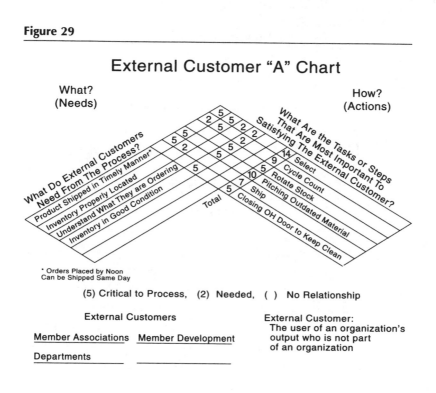

What?
(Needs)

How?
(Actions)

* Orders Placed by Noon
Can be Shipped Same Day

(5) Critical to Process, (2) Needed, ( ) No Relationship

External Customers

Member Associations   Member Development

Departments

External Customer:
The user of an organization's
output who is not part
of an organization

Figure 30

Internal Customer "A" Chart

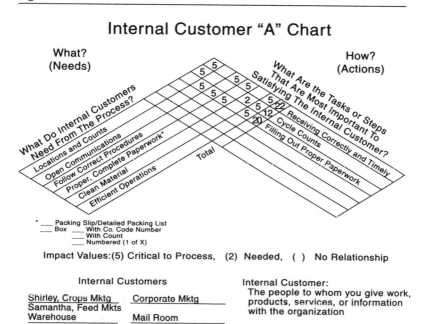

What?
(Needs)

How?
(Actions)

* ___ Packing Slip/Detailed Packing List
___ Box ___ With Co. Code Number
___ With Count
___ Numbered (1 of X)

Impact Values:(5) Critical to Process, (2) Needed, ( ) No Relationship

Internal Customers

Shirley, Crops Mktg   Corporate Mktg
Samantha, Feed Mkts
Warehouse   Mail Room

Internal Customer:
The people to whom you give work,
products, services, or information
with the organization

CRITICAL CONTROL POINTS

Figure 31

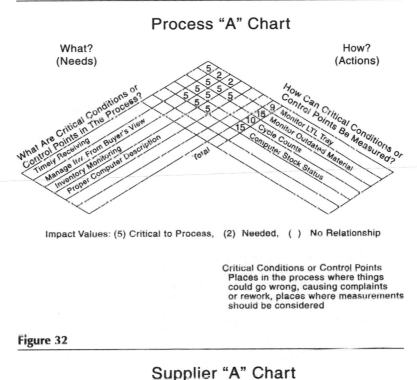

Process "A" Chart

Impact Values: (5) Critical to Process,   (2) Needed,   ( )   No Relationship

Critical Conditions or Control Points
Places in the process where things
could go wrong, causing complaints
or rework, places where measurements
should be considered

Figure 32

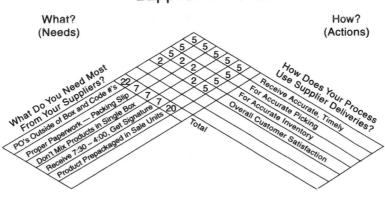

Supplier "A" Chart

Impact Values: (5) Critical to Process,   (2) Needed,   ( )   No Relationship

Suppliers	
Corporate Mktg	Milestone Press
Falkenberge	Blue Mile Grass
Print Shop	Color Line Wheel
The Printing Co	

Supplier:
Any process or person who
provides inputs to the process

Tools, Equipment, and Supplies:

1. Cleaning equipment
2. Dust covers
3. Packing supplies

Figure 33

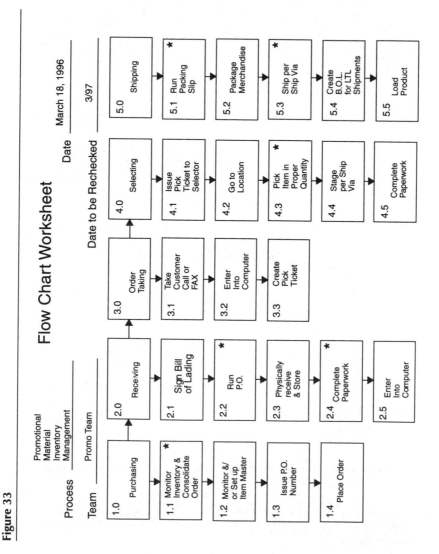

Flow Chart Worksheet

Process Promotional Material Inventory Management

Team Promo Team

Date March 18, 1996

Date to be Rechecked 3/97

1.0 Purchasing
1.1 Monitor Inventory & Consolidate Order *
1.2 Monitor &/ or Set up Item Master
1.3 Issue P.O. Number
1.4 Place Order

2.0 Receiving
2.1 Sign Bill of Lading
2.2 Run P.O. *
2.3 Physically receive & Store
2.4 Complete Paperwork *
2.5 Enter Into Computer

3.0 Order Taking
3.1 Take Customer Call or FAX
3.2 Enter Into Computer
3.3 Create Pick Ticket

4.0 Selecting
4.1 Issue Pick Ticket to Selector
4.2 Go to Location
4.3 Pick Item in Proper Quantity *
4.4 Stage per Ship Via
4.5 Complete Paperwork

5.0 Shipping
5.1 Run Packing Slip *
5.2 Package Merchandise
5.3 Ship per Ship Via *
5.4 Create B.O.L. for LTL Shipments
5.5 Load Product

Table 1. Key Steps Analysis For: Promotional Support Material Inventory Management

Key Step No.	Key Step Name	Best Known Way	Tricks of The Trade	Consequences
1.1	Monitor inventory and consolidate order	Stock position Rept Past sales history Spot counts Adjustments Seasonal monitor	Lead time eliminates crisis	Could run out of product
1.3	Issue P.O. number	Enter into computer Type selector note to dispose of all old inventory before receiving as applicable		Mixing out-dated with current inventory

1.4	Place order	Administrative Asst. contacts Vendor, Corporate Marketing, Promotions, and/or Lab Manager, depending on product line (see attached list)
		
		Info we communicate to the vendor:
		1. P.O. #
		2. Description
		3. Quantity-packs
		4. Count/pack
		5. Ship to address
		6. Delivery date
		7. Whs receiving time is 7:30 a.m. - 3:00 p.m.
		Communicate the following shipping requirements to the vendor:
		1. Packing slip
		  – P.O. #
		  – Description
		  – Quantity-number of packs
		2. Info on box(s)
		  – P.O. #
		  – Code #
		  – Description
		  – Number of packs/box
		  – Count/pack
			Be sure to include Bldg. 1 in address	• Difficulty in receiving
				• Delivered to the wrong building

2.2	Run P.O.	Type P.O. number into the computer - print receiving document	If P.O. not in system receive by code number and existing locations	Untimely receiving and lost product
2.4	Complete paperwork	Fill out receiving report correctly and return to office	Verify the quantity-packs, eaches, etc.	Wrong or mis-located inventory
4.3	Pick item in proper quantity	Go to proper location, verify code number and description, pick quantity by pack		• Wrong product or quantity shipped • Wrong inventory

5.1	Run packing slip	Enter pick ticket number. Make needed changes-back order product, cancel, update inventory, location change		Customer won't be billed Changes in inventory status won't be made
5.3	Ship per ship via	Physically verify ship via on packing slip	Proliferation of ship vias complicates this area • Known deadline for shipment • Billing for freight	Shipped incorrectly

Exceptions:	When supplier has a rush shipment, Shirley will call Jay personally to alert him that a rush order is being delivered and it may be after normal warehouse receiving hours.

Measurement:	We will monitor accuracy of inventory through cycle counts.
Cycle Counts:	Shirley fax count request to Jay. Count and adjustment made within 24 hours. Request faxed back to Shirley when complete.

March 13, 1996
(PROMOPM.P37)

Attachment

Administrative Assistant in Crops Division will order:

Sign Posts, Nuts/Bolts, Flag Markers

Work with others on:

Seed Signs—James O'Keife

Seed Stickers—Dave Turnnell, Sam Williamson

Pens—Sue Holtes

Soil Sample Bags—Jeff Kraft

Soil Test Mailing Bags—Jeff Kraft

Soil Test Request Forms—Jeff Kraft

Jeff Kraft in Central Lab will order:

Forage and Feed Mailing Kits, Plant Analysis Sample Kits

James O'Keife in Corporate Marketing will order:

All others

Process Master

For

Separating Waste Oils

Process Master #42

Date: September 15, 1997

Our process master team has identified and written down the best known ways to carry out our process. By signing below, I agree to follow the attached process master whenever possible. I understand that exceptional situations may force a temporary change in the process. When this happens, I will act in the best interests of my customers. I will also turn in a Process Master Exception Report of the temporary changes for possible updating of the process master.

Team Sponsor:	Sam Guzman
Team Leader:	Bob Gibbs
Process Team Members:	Ron Durrance
	Andy Alban
	Jerry Spurgeon
	Steve Dajani
	Bill Keys

Date of Revisions: Expected September, 1998

Group Norms:

1. Everyone will participate

2. Phone calls and pages will wait till meeting is done

3. We will start on time

4. We will support the process master

5. Honesty, sharing, considerate, polite behavior

6. Meeting time is 8:45 to 9:30 every Tuesday in Green Conference Room

7. Andy Alban will be the scribe and bring meeting supplies.

Figure 34

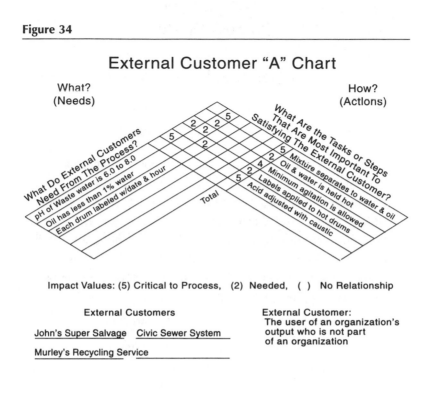

External Customer "A" Chart

What?
(Needs)

How?
(Actions)

Impact Values: (5) Critical to Process, (2) Needed, ( ) No Relationship

External Customers

John's Super Salvage   Civic Sewer System

Murley's Recycling Service

External Customer:
The user of an organization's
output who is not part
of an organization

Figure 35

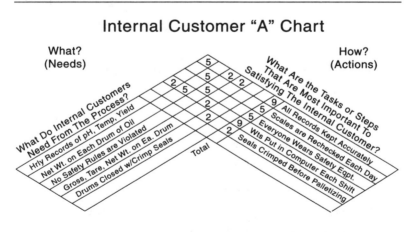

Internal Customer "A" Chart

What?
(Needs)

How?
(Actions)

Impact Values: (5) Critical to Process, (2) Needed, ( ) No Relationship

Internal Customers

Wastewater, J. Martin   Safety, R. Louis

Accounting, E. Hardy   Shipping, J. Dorman

Internal Customer:
The people to whom you give work,
products, services, or information
within the organization

CRITICAL CONTROL POINTS

Figure 36

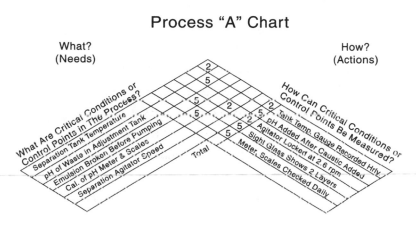

Process "A" Chart

Impact Values: (5) Critical to Process, (2) Needed, ( ) No Relationship

Critical Conditions or Control Points:
Places in the process where things
could go wrong, causing complaints
or rework, places where measurements
should be considered

Figure 37

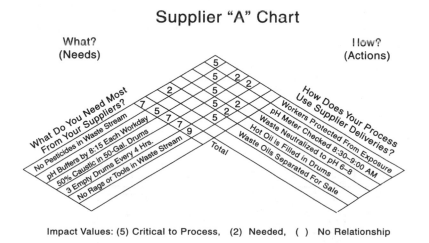

Supplier "A" Chart

Impact Values: (5) Critical to Process, (2) Needed, ( ) No Relationship

Suppliers		Supplier:
Mix dept, C. Adams	Max Chemical Co	Any process or person who provides inputs to the process
QC Lab, C. Armstrong	Receiving, K. Kuzneckis	

Tools, Equipment, Supplies

1. 2 inch aluminum Bung wrench

2. 2 inch seal crimper

3. Pocket pH meter—Orion Mini 46B with plastic combination electrode

4. Digital scales—Albertson Excel 1000 lb.

5. Portable Diaphragm Pump—Clover 888

6. Calibrated 5 gallon stainless bucket

7. Face shield, rubber apron, & 18" gloves

8. pH 7.0 and 4.0 buffer solutions

9. 2" Bung seals

10. 55 gallon blue plastic drums—Mansco 605

11. 8" x 3" white label blanks

12. 40 ml disposable plastic beakers.

Figure 38

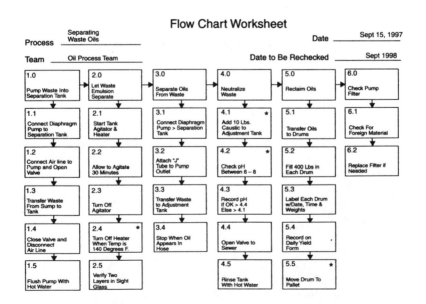

Flow Chart Worksheet

Table 2. Key Steps Analysis for Separating Waste Oils

Key Step No.	Key Step Name	Best Known Way	Tricks of The Trade	Consequences
2.4	Turn off heater when temp is 140°F		Usually takes 25–30 minutes	Too cool, plugs pump. Too hot, burned fingers.
4.1	Add 10 lbs. caustic to adjustment tank	Weigh caustic in stainless pail. Pour in slowly.	Wear full face mask, apron and gloves.	Burns
4.2	Check pH between 6-8	Dip out 5-10 ml in 40 ml beaker, 5 or more minutes after adding caustic.	Wear full face mask, apron and gloves.	Burns
5.5	Move drum to pallet			Broken pallet

Exceptions:	If equipment fails to work, call supervisor. Office: 102 Home: 421-0202.			
Measurement:	Temperature	- Gauge on side of separation tank	140°F	+/- 1°F
	pH	- Pocket pH meter in 40 ml beaker	7.0	+/- 1.0

September 18, 1997
(PROMOPM.P42)

References

AT&T (1989). *Process Quality Management & Improvement Guidelines.* Publication Center AT&T Bell Laboratories.

Dickenson, T. (1995). "Keep Track of Your Measures by Using A Measures Data Base." *Quality Progress.* September, 1995: p. 168.

Finn, L., with S. Reynard, C. Garhart (1995). *Managing For Quality.* Joiner Associates Incorporated, Issue Number 12 — Fall 1995.

Fitz-enz, J. (1995). *How To Measure Resources Management.* New York: McGraw-Hill, Second Edition. p. 263.

Goldratt, E. (1996). *Managing & Implementing Change.* Quality Satellite Network, Spring Satellite Seminars. May 9, 1996. Tele No. 800-333-4152.

Haller, H. S., Ph.D.: President, Harold S Haller & Company, Cleveland, 1997.

Harbour, J. L., Ph.D. (1997). *The Basics of Performance Measurement.* New York: Quality Resources, p. 23–24.

Chapter 6

SPECIAL APPLICATIONS OF PROCESS MASTERING

There are many demands placed on organizations. These include government requirements as well as self-imposed initiatives such as ISO certification and quality initiatives. Every organization is resource-constrained so everyone looks for methods and opportunities to accomplish multiple demands as efficiently as possible. Whenever possible it is desirable to accomplish two or more requirements at the same time. Such might be the case if your business is required to meet OSHA process safety regulations, EPA's risk management plans, as well as ISO 9002 requirements. We believe you should be able to do a process master and meet more than one requirement.

What follows is a description of possible applications of process mastering in three areas that could overlap. The reader will have to determine the fine details of applicability in each case and modify the process master approach as necessary to meet regulatory requirements.

HACCP and Process Mastering

Those of you in the food processing industry will be aware of the meaning of the letters HACCP. For the rest, Hazard Analysis of Critical Control Points may be news. HACCP follows scientific principles and includes training, monitoring, and auditing to prevent toxins, foreign materials, and harmful chemicals from entering the food supply. Traditional quality control methods have depended upon random sampling of final products to ensure safe foods. HACCP methods focus on prevention of problems from the production of raw materials through food processing operations and shipping to the consumer.

A background understanding of worldwide efforts to improve the food supply is important. Borders are becoming meaningless in the trade of foods between countries. Domestic standards and systems of compliance for foods and other products undergo international scrutiny and are sometimes considered technical barriers to free trade. Risk management has become a first-priority competitive factor, and a strong food-safety focus is required in the management of product liability. HACCP is recognized worldwide as an effective tool for ensuring food safety. A supplier with a working HACCP system will have a competitive advantage over one without HACCP in place.

The World Health Organization, Codex Alimentarius, the World Trade Organization, the General Agreement on Tariffs and Trade, and the International Organization for Standardization have started to discuss requirement of HACCP compliance for foods traded in international commerce. Equivalent process standards and practices are expected to be developed and followed worldwide.

The U.S. Food and Drug Administration (FDA) lists food safety hazards that are reasonably likely to occur and must be controlled: natural toxins, microbial contamination, chemical contamination, pesticides, drug residues, decomposition, unapproved additives, and physical hazards. Not all categories will apply to each location, so each food processor must know its product and process in order to limit the list of hazards to be assessed in the HACCP plan. According to Paula Kurtzwell of FDA, a typical HACCP plan involves seven steps:

1. *Analyze hazards* associated with foods. The hazards might include biological (such as spoilage or toxins), chemicals (such as mercury and PCBs), or physical (such as glass or metal fragments).

2. *Identify Critical Control points* places in the process where the hazards can be controlled or measured

3. *Establish critical limits* for each measurement at critical points. Examples might include pH, cook time, and temperature or freezer temperature.

4. *Establish ways to monitor control points* such as when, how, and by whom the critical control points will be measured.

5. *Establish corrective actions to be taken* if and when a critical limit has been exceeded. Examples are reprocessing or disposing of the food if the minimum cook temperature has not been met.

6. *Establish effective recordkeeping systems* to show compliance with the plan.

7. *Establish auditing procedures* to be sure the system is working consistently, such as auditing production and cooking records to be sure all the critical limits have been met for the production run.

Many companies view HACCP as a part of their total quality management initiative, and see it as a good, commonsense business practice. Early efforts to set up a working HACCP system were long and painful. Companies became discouraged and dropped out. However, with the use of new tools such as process mastering, the time and complexity to implement a working HACCP program can be reduced and made easier. If you want to apply process mastering to HACCP, it is vital to choose the correct team members.

A specialized steering team is needed for this important work. The *Guide to US Food Safety Law* lists these team members: a microbiologist, a toxicologist, a regulatory specialist, an engineer, a production specialist, and a quality assurance specialist (Mancini, 84). In the real world, however, most team members will have to do double duty. At most small food processing companies, one full-time microbiologist or food scientist is needed to identify the control points and oversee the program. Food microbiologists and toxicologists at the local university can be called for advice. Small companies can also call on the Food Safety Consortium, American Meat Institute, the Center for Food Safety and Quality Enhancement, or the National Food Processors Association for assistance.

One person must be designated as overall food safety coordinator and this person needs to have full-time responsibility for the HACCP program. According to Bob Strong, president of ASI Food Safety Consultants, HACCP means more planning and investigation than traditional quality assurance (Mancini, 86). If HACCP and quality assurance responsibilities are combined, the company needs to be sure the HACCP coordinator does not get involved in day-to-day product testing. Other members of the HACCP team include representatives from purchasing, sanitation supervision, maintenance supervision, a refrigeration specialist, a production specialist, and quality assurance. A team sponsor within the HACCP team is important to be sure the team is supported with secretarial help, meeting facilities and management assistance, as needed. The team members should be able to communicate well with management and workers, and one or more should be able to train workers.

MASTERING A PROCESS WITH HACCP REQUIREMENTS

Process mastering can provide a framework for establishing and standardizing safe processes. Mastering a process under a HACCP system means making a few modifications to the standard process mastering steps.

Step 1: Select a team leader

The sponsor from the HACCP steering team selects a team leader. The team leader requirements should include food safety training.

Step 2: Define the process

A process should be defined with thought to where critical control points affect food safety. *Process masters must be written to standardize the methods where critical control points guard employee or customer safety.*

Step 3: Select a team

This step should include selection of the actual operators where the process includes HACCP critical control points. Temporary team members should include the HACCP coordinator, plant engineer, microbiologist, regulatory specialist, or other technical experts to discuss the critical control points and possible food hazards. Temporary team members may attend only a meeting or two, in steps five, six, and seven.

Step 4: Establish team norms

No change needed here.

Step 5: Flow chart the process

It may be necessary to add key process steps in order to measure or control critical control points. (This is a change from the process mastering rule prohibiting addition of steps where no one was doing the step before.) Because it is related to safety, be sure to mark every key process step where a critical control point is measured or controlled. Every key process step will be captured (standardized) in step ten.

Step 6: List the customers' needs and process interactions

It is important to discuss the reasons (theory) behind the HACCP food safety requirements in this step. An expert in food safety should be present to answer any questions. The maintenance supervisor or plant engineer may also be present to discuss the capability of the equipment, if needed. The HACCP food safety requirements area should be listed on the left side of the "A" chart with the customers' needs. For example, some food safety requirements might include:

1. Product is free from foreign material.
2. Spoilage has not been allowed to contaminate the product.
3. Pesticides used in the plant are not allowed to enter the product.

On the right side of the "A" chart, the team should list the process actions contributing to safe products. Expert knowledge should be utilized to help the team determine safety requirements and list process safeguards.

Step 7: List what is controlled in the process

Critical control points will probably show up here. They should be listed on the left side of the "A" chart. Examples of these critical control points may include:

1. Freezer temperature
2. Cooking time and temperature
3. pH
4. Viscosity
5. Double-seam overlap
6. Reactor pressure
7. *E. coli* presence

Methods used to monitor the safe operation of the process should be listed on the right side of the "A" chart. Actions to control these critical control points will need to be standardized.

Step 8: List needs from suppliers and how they will be used

For this step, the team should list microbiological, chemical and physical hazards to be absent from raw materials and supplies, such as:

1. Eggs are free from Salmonella
2. Fruit is free from harmful foreign material and rot.

Step 9: List tools, equipment, and supplies

No change is needed here.

Step 9½: Double-check the process

The HACCP process specialist and food safety expert(s) should go over the ongoing process master carefully together, to be certain no critical control points have been missed.

Step 10: Capture key steps

The appropriate HACCP team members should attend this process mastering meeting. They should discuss any additional steps needed to meet HACCP requirements. Where the process mastering team has developed a consensus about the best known way to do an existing step, HACCP team members should examine the step from a food-safety viewpoint. If a key process step needs to be established or modified, in order to measure or control a critical control point, the team needs to discuss how best to carry out the step. (This is an exception to the rule; in this case it is acceptable to create a step and insert it into the process.) When filling in the Key Step Worksheet, the team needs to be sure to capture the consequences (hazards) of doing it wrong. Exceptions to the rules should always include suggested actions to be taken for any deviations outside the critical control point limits. The team should agree on critical control point measurements, methods and targets with limits.

Step 11: Try out the process master

Workers in the process need to be trained in the best known way of doing the process, as usual. In addition, the process workers will need to understand the HACCP system. This means all the plant workers will eventually need to be trained to follow the HACCP requirements. A typical eight-hour training session is described in "Worker Training" below.

Step 12: Review the trial and modify the process master

No change is needed.

Step 13: Complete and sign off

No change.

Monitor use

No change.

WORKER TRAINING

HACCP requires extra training for the workers who are to be involved in food processing, shipping, or storage. Plant workers need to understand the hazards and how they are to be controlled and monitored. The members of the HACCP team should lead the training sessions, if possible. About eight hours of initial practical training is needed on these subjects:

1. Introduction, history, and company intent to follow a rigorous HACCP program. Food safety examples should be based on the workers' own experiences, if possible.

2. Analysis of biological, chemical, and physical hazards. Good manufacturing practices videotapes can be shown and actual work examples discussed.

3. Critical control points in the workers' process are discussed. This is a good time to discuss the importance of process masters as a foundation for control point measurements.

4. Measurements in the workers' process should be discussed. This might include how, where, when, and by whom the process will be measured.

5. Critical limits are to be discussed. Targets and limits in the workers' process should be explained.

6. The team should discuss with the workers the corrective actions to be taken and by whom. Care should be taken to prevent worsening the situation because of inappropriate corrective action (tampering with the process).

7. Written records and automatic charts should be discussed, along with how the records will be used to improve the process.

8. Auditing methods should be discussed to be sure everyone from first to last understands that the HACCP program must work properly every day to produce safe food products, not only on auditing days.

OLD PROCESS MASTERS VS. NEW HACCP REQUIREMENTS

Where processes have been mastered before starting a HACCP system, the HACCP requirements may necessitate some changes to the process. The processes should be re-mastered with the appropriate food safety issues in mind. Actually, this is preferable to starting a new HACCP system from the ground up, because the process mastering teams will have become accustomed to thinking about customer needs, will be working together to make team decisions and will have standardized the most critical process steps. Where process masters have been done in food-safety related processes, the process workers are usually aware of food safety issues, and this will require less training.

Where no processes have been standardized with standard operating procedures or process masters, we recommend that only the processes related to HACCP critical control points be mastered first, then progressing to the noncritical processes as time permits. Because the processes are being standardized for the first time, many suggestions will be generated in the process mastering phase. A large number of suggestions may tend to bury the maintenance and other departments in work orders. There is a real danger of losing momentum if suggestions are not answered in less than a month.

Process mastering can aid in establishing a comprehensive HACCP system. The workers are usually willing to help standardize their processes in order to enable them to do better work. HACCP builds on this foundation, and can be done more easily where effective process standards already exist.

ISO 9000 and Process Mastering

Before understanding how valuable process mastering is to achieving ISO 9000 registration, it is important to understand what ISO 9000 includes. If you already understand ISO 9000, feel free to skip to "Process Mastering Can Turbocharge the Registration Process," later in this section. The rest of us will cover the basics on ISO, here.

Many companies are joining the parade to ISO 9000 registration. As of this writing, more than 15,000 U.S. companies and more than 45,000 European companies have been registered since 1992. The important question is: "Why spend the time and capital to be registered in ISO or any other voluntary quality standard?" It is important to understand what ISO is and is not, before you decide if the value is there for your company.

Kenneth S. Stevens defines ISO 9000 as "a uniform, consistent set of procedures, elements, and requirements for quality assurance that can be applied universally to any total quality system." It has been adopted by more than 125 countries and many large companies in order to improve the quality of goods and services nationally and internationally. ISO has been used to meet customer demands for a basic quality system and to start on a total quality system that has long-term benefits to the entire firm.

The ISO series is not a standard for total quality. It does not describe the quality of any product. It does not address continuous improvement, or whether firms are adept at delighting customers. Its adoption does not ensure the long-term survival of a company. Companies who adopt ISO often spend years in the process of becoming certified, spending tens of thousands of dollars per location for the privilege.

Why do so many companies go to the trouble and expense to become registered? To answer this tough question, we should understand ISO's background, areas covered, the registration process, and how process mastering has been used to shorten the time and cut the cost of registration.

BACKGROUND AND DESCRIPTION OF ISO 9000

ISO 9000 is a system of quality assurance guidelines that was written to enhance international harmony, trade, cooperation, and business opportunities. It is a set of standards for a basic quality system. ISO 9000 has its roots in many international quality standards, including Mil-Q-9858A.

The governing body that writes and revises the standards is the International Organization for Standardization. The first set (Phase I) was adopted by the European community in 1987, in order to reduce inspections, quality disputes, and customs delays between European countries. ISO 9000 was rapidly adopted by more than 125 countries around the world. Many firms now insist that their suppliers conform to ISO documentation standards as a business requirement.

ISO 9000 is an umbrella term for four levels of quality assurance competence. ISO 9000-1 *Quality Management and Quality Assurance Standards - Part I: Guidelines for Selection and Use* consists of an introduction, definitions, types of standards (9001–9004), selection of a quality assurance model, precontract assessment, tailoring, and reviewing a contract and a cross-referenced list of quality system elements. ISO 9001, 9002, and 9003 describe degrees of demonstration that a customer may require of a supplier. They are levels of quality assurance above the minimum (9004).

ISO 9001 is for use when conformance to specified needs is to be assured by the supplier throughout the whole product cycle, from design to servicing. This level includes assurance of 20 quality requirements at their most stringent level, as well as meeting the requirements of 9002, 9003, and 9004.

ISO 9002 demonstrates a competent level of assurance for production, installation, and servicing. It is the same as 9001, except design control is not addressed. 9002 also includes the requirements for 9003 and 9004.

ISO 9003 applies to situations in which only the supplier's capabilities for product inspection and test methods must be demonstrated. It includes the requirements for 9004.

ISO 9004 is intended to serve as a guideline for developing a basic quality system. It describes more than 90 quality system elements. A manufacturer can pick the appropriate elements in order to maximize quality assurance effectiveness at minimum cost.

ISO 9000 Preparation and Certification

According to Zaciewski, a fundamental step is selection of the appropriate ISO standard—9001, 9002, or 9003. The easiest decision is to match your customers' required registration level. If not, your management team should examine the ISO standards and compare them to your customers' needs, analysis of your competitors' strengths and weaknesses, analysis of your firm's quality performance, and whether your firm plans to initiate a total quality process in the future.

A decision to seek ISO registration is a serious decision involving both time and money. Time should be spent analyzing the costs and benefits. A quality function deployment matrix may be helpful at this point to focus on areas where your firm may not meet the standard's requirements. We recommend the use of a decision matrix such as those used in *Better Designs in Half the Time: Implementing Quality Function Deployment in America,* by Bob King.

The senior management team and a quality expert need to assess customer requirements and the firm's capabilities to determine whether to proceed and at what ISO registration level.

The team assesses how well each element of the quality assurance system fulfills each of the requirements of the ISO standard. An impartial expert should be employed to determine effectiveness of the present quality system. Deficiencies should be listed and plans made for upgrading systems. Assessment checklists are also helpful for training the team members. Checklists are widely available in book and software formats.

This pre-assessment will show any gaps between the ISO requirements and the current quality system. Early performance of this internal assessment will aid in strategic planning, budgeting, and improvement efforts prior to involving a consultant in the ISO registration program.

Once the decision is made to proceed with ISO registration, an internal ISO coordinator is selected for ISO training and to lead the preparation/registration process. The coordinator or designee trains each department head in the ISO requirements and auditing procedures.

Each department head is charged with responsibility for development of specification documents, procedures, and instructions for each process bearing on quality and for record-keeping. Information exchange between departments is especially critical in the areas of quality and customer needs.

Each critical process must be mapped, written, and followed by each operator. In our experience with manufacturing processes, each location had at least 150 critical processes that were mapped and written by the department personnel. (No one likes to write down job instructions, but processes drift toward comfort and away from original intent if not kept in writing.) Accurate in-process and finished-product records are required for ISO compliance.

When the organization's processes have been documented and accurate records are the norm, formal internal audits are performed with reports to management. Any discrepancies are noted, and corrective actions are undertaken.

When the quality assurance system is believed to meet the ISO requirements, a certified ISO registrar is brought into the process. The registrar will assess the quality system and report any corrections that may be needed. Many organizations that have not mastered their processes commonly fail to meet all the ISO requirements on the first audit. A second or third visit by the auditor may be needed before registration is achieved.

The time from a decision to start until ISO registration is achieved commonly varies between one and three years. This time depends to a great extent upon the quality environment in place within each organization. Companies with some total quality experience can usually achieve registration more easily. Companies having less experience with quality practices will take longer.

PROCESS MASTERING CAN TURBOCHARGE THE REGISTRATION PROCESS

You may remember our earlier discussion of Process Masters at Integral Ingredients (Chapter 5). Because of the quality environment in place at Integral, the company was able to race to ISO registration at light speed.

In 1991, Integral Ingredients decided to roll out a total quality improvement (TQI) process in order to better serve its 3,500 industrial customers. The TQI process had short-term, mid-term, and long-term elements, including process mastering, Supplier-Customer Partnerships, and Deming's 14 Points for Management.

Process mastering was used to stabilize processes and identify variation between workers doing the same jobs. The senior management team saw the value in process mastering early in 1992, and each department was asked to list processes to be mastered in their areas. More than 220 processes were listed. The management team saw that this number of processes would be impossible to complete in a reasonable time, so they asked the department heads to cut the list to only those where the process:

1. is directly related to customer needs, or

2. is related to employee or product safety, or

3. is error-prone or has wide variations in output, or

4. is where process improvements are planned.

This list was shorter—only 180 processes. The quality improvement coordinator trained 18 team sponsors, who worked with one or two teams at a time until all 180 processes were completed. This phase of the TQI process required 26 months and resulted in numerous process improvements.

During that period, the sample-order delivery cycle dropped from 14 days to 3 days. The production-delivery cycle was shortened several times, from 10 days to 6 days. The on-time shipment rate jumped from 56 percent on-time to 91 percent on-time. Production volume in this time period increased by 49 percent, with a 21 percent increase in production workers. Production of scrap material was cut in half.

In 1994, it became apparent that ISO 9002 registration would be a selling point, so the decision was made to get registered as soon as possible. An ISO coordinator from each location was trained, and a quality policy was written by the senior managers. The coordinators developed a quality manual and forms for each specification and procedure.

Each department head was trained in ISO 9000 procedures, and every department wrote specifications and procedures for each process within the department. Because 180 process masters had been written, it was a simple matter to include them

> "Informal surveys of hundreds of companies—from multinationals to the smallest shops—indicate that a major people component of the ISO 9000 process is often missed in an effort to gain certification: Employees don't write the work procedures.
> Instead, consultants write the work procedures and produce the obligatory quality manual. Therefore, the positive change that results from involving employees never happens."
>
> Amy Zuckerman
> Alan Hurwitz

by way of reference. Process masters were considered Level 3 documents or work instructions. As such, they became part of the overall document control system. Sign-off by the team sponsor took on additional meaning as approval by an authorized person. And measurement/monitoring data were now considered part of ISO quality records. This enabled the ISO team to start internal department audits within six months of the starting date.

By the eighth month, a team of registrars had audited each Integral location. One location had one minor deficiency. That correction was made and Integral received a recommendation that they be registered. They wrote in their letter that the prewritten process masters had enabled Integral to be approved in the shortest time to date.

The registration certificates arrived at Integral late in the tenth month. Normally, the process takes 18 to 24 months and costs $15–25,000. At Integral Ingredients, it took ten months and $8,000. Integral's president gave credit for the quick registration to the teams who had completed the process masters.

The bottom line for Integral Ingredients was that process mastering helped ISO registration go much more quickly and smoothly. Integral had an ongoing total quality improvement system as well as ISO 9002 registration.

Other Process Mastering Applications

Several other classes of standards have been and will be developed. They cover many processes that are good candidates for using process mastering. Some of the standards and sponsoring organizations are listed here, although many more are omitted:

QS-9000, developed in 1994 by the Chrysler, Ford, and General Motors Supplier Quality Requirements Task Force, based on the ISO 9000 standards.

The *TE-9000* supplement to QS-9000, developed by Chrysler, Ford, and General Motors for tooling and equipment suppliers of nonproduction parts.

ISO 14000, Environmental Management Standards, under development by the International Organization for Standardization.

Malcolm Baldrige National Quality Award and numerous state quality awards.

Processes related to:

The Bureau of Motor Vehicles

Occupational Safety and Health Administration

Environmental Protection Agency

United States Department of Agriculture

Federal Emergency Management Agency

Food and Drug Administration

Federal Communications Commission

Federal Trade Commission

National Labor Relations Board

Joint Council on Accreditation of Healthcare
    Organizations.

Safety and Process Mastering

Every year in this country, thousands of individuals are injured both on and off the job. In 1992 there were 8,100,000 disabling injuries and 40,000 deaths. The true cost to the nation for only the work-related deaths and injuries was estimated by the National Safety Council to be $115.9 billion in 1992. The tremendous cost in dollars and suffering should be uppermost in everybody's mind. The federal government through the Occupational Safety and Health Administration (OSHA) has been required for many years to assist industry in bringing down this tremendous loss to our economy and citizens. In 1992, OSHA published a regulation entitled *Process Safety Management of Highly Hazardous Chemicals*, 29 CFR 1910.119. This regulation applies to only those industries that handle specific highly hazardous chemicals above a threshold quantity. Within the regulation are requirements that are very similar to process mastering. Put another way, process masters may well address many of the requirements of this regulation.

Among other things, the regulation calls for written analysis of processes. It requires employee participation. It requires process flowcharting and hazard identification. When things go wrong (exceptions) it requires incident investigations. Audits must be performed on the program's implementation, its effectiveness, and its improvement. And the regulation requires a regimen of training: initial, refresher, and for outside contractors. These requirements, of course, are all covered in the parts of any process master.

When the subject of safety is looked at in a broader context, not just a specific OSHA regulation, it will be obvious that process mastering can be very useful to analyze specific dangerous processes. Any employer who truly cares about his/her employees will want to give them the opportunity to do their jobs more safely. This approach can be used on the well-known dangerous activities such as lockout/tagout, confined space entry, and hot work jobs. But beyond the already identified dangerous processes, there are many unknown risks. To look further for the most important process to analyze from a safety perspective, consider the following categories of activities.

NONROUTINE AND UNUSUAL TASKS

These jobs pop up only occasionally or are a one-of-a-kind situation. These situations may arise in production or nonproduction settings.

NONPRODUCTION ACTIVITIES

These jobs or processes are usually in maintenance or research and development.

CERTAIN CONSTRUCTION ACTIVITIES

Examples include scaffolding, temporary electrical circuits and equipment, trenching operations, elevated work assignments, steel erection, and similar activities.

HIGH ENERGY SOURCES AND RELEASES

Whenever people are working with energy sources such as electricity, steam, compressed gases, flammable liquids and gases, and hydraulics, they are at risk if the danger is not recognized and planned for.

Process mastering should also be used on the more mundane, everyday processes where risks are not so obvious. In fact, we suggest that "safety" should be taken out of the realm of "extra" and brought into the mainstream of thought and action. If processes are mastered as suggested in this book, safety will be an integral part of how a process is performed. The employees who know the hazards best will have considered them and will have decided on how the task can be done safely. Approached in this manner, safety is given an entirely new perspective.

Here is one closing thought on the subject of safety. Most companies have a safety department or at least someone who has the extra responsibility for safety. Many companies have a quality department or someone designated to be in charge of quality. We have come to the conclusion that safety, or risk management, as some people refer to it, and quality are the opposite sides of the same coin. In fact, if the business is run using a continuous improvement approach, both blend into the daily routine and are no longer special. They are the best known way to run a business.

References

King, B. (1989). *Better Designs in Half the Time: Implementing Quality Function Deployment in America*. Methuen: Goal/QPC.

Mancini, L. (1994). "Drafting the HACCP Team." *Food Engineering*. November 1994: pp. 83–88.

Stevens, K. S. (1994). "ISO 9000 and Total Quality." *Quality Management Journal*. Fall 1994: pp. 57–71.

Zaciewski, R. D. (1995). "ISO 9000 Preparation: The First Crucial Steps." *Quality Progress*, ASQC, Milwaukee: November 1995: pp. 81–83.

Zuckerman, A., A. Hurwitz (1996). "How Companies Miss the Boat on ISO 9000." *Quality Progress*, ASQC, Milwaukee: July 1996: 7: p. 23.

Chapter 7

CLOSING WORDS

Recently one of the authors attended an annual luncheon for retirees of his former company. He was struck by the appearance and demeanor of all the retirees who had departed the company within the last six to eight months. They all looked healthy, more relaxed, and happy than he had ever seen them. Some of these people had spent most of their work lives in offices; others in warehouses and manufacturing plants. There was no distinction between them. They all looked better.

The same author, at a church discussion group where people with an average age of 50 were discussing their dreams and expectations of retirement, was amazed at the overwhelming desire expressed by the participants to get out of their present jobs. Few, it seemed, really liked what they were doing. They didn't like what they had to go through to do their jobs. This group was made up primarily of professionals such as physicians, chemists, psychologists, attorneys, and business leaders.

> "I'm a machine," says the spot-welder. "I'm caged," says the bank teller, and echoes the hotel clerk. "I'm a mule," says the steelworker. "I'm less than a farm implement," says the migrant worker. "I'm an object," says the high-fashion model.
>
> Studs Terkel

> "Process centering changes all this. Your work may still largely consist of tightening bolts or handling forms, but now you have a sense of control and influence over it. You are a responsible actor in your own work drama; you make choices and you make a difference."
>
> Michael Hammer

We don't believe this is the way it has to be. Csikszentmihalyi says we are most happy when our "body or mind is stretched to its limits in a voluntary effort to accomplish something difficult and worthwhile." Isn't this what organizations are or should be asking of and providing for their employees? If they did, wouldn't it be a win-win situation for all parties?

A major message in Deming's theory of management is directed toward allowing workers to have joy in work. He says we must show people what their jobs are and how their work fits in with others in the system. When this happens, the workers can engage their minds and their labor, and they will have joy in their work.

Michael Hammer, in the final chapter of his book, *Beyond Reengineering*, says, "Even the most mundane work can be given meaning and value for those who perform it if they understand how it benefits, even in the simplest of ways, the lives of others. Process-centered work can help satisfy everyone's hunger for connection with something beyond themselves and their own needs. It widens our horizons and connects us with others—with our teammates, with our organization, with our customers. In the process-centered world, dignity is restored to work, the dignity that was lost to workers who only performed repetitive tasks."

Process mastering allows workers, as part of a team, to shape and understand their work, to see its inherent worth as part of a larger system, and to do the work with quality and intensity that is worthy of their personal investment.

When workers are given good, challenging work to do, when they have the opportunity to do it in cooperation with others, and when they have some choice and control over how it is done, they are more likely to have joy in their work. For many people, helping to master a process may be the first time they have ever had the opportunity to change their work situation. We believe, when they do, their life will change and their organization will benefit.

References

Csikszentmihalyi, M. (1990). *Flow—The Psychology of Optimal Experience*. New York: Harper Perennial, p. 3.

Deming, W. E. (1993). *The New Economics; For Industry, Government, Education*. Cambridge: MIT Center For Advanced Engineering Study, p. 61.

Hammer, M. (1996). *Beyond Reengineering*. New York: HarperBusiness, p. 268.

Terkel, S. (1972, 1974). *Working*. New York: Ballantine Books, 1972, 1974: p. xiv.

Appendix A

PROCESS MASTERING FORMS

Figure A-1

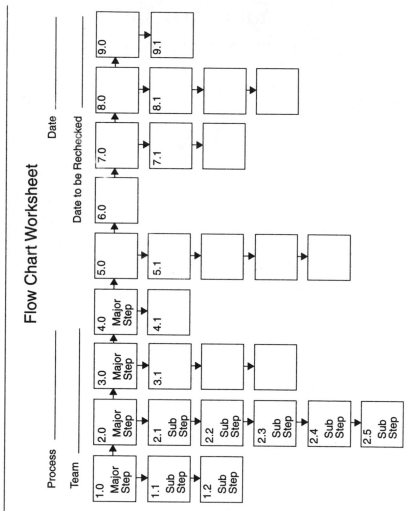

Figure A-2

External Customer "A" Chart

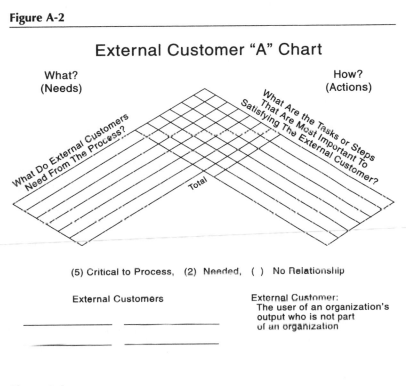

What?
(Needs)

How?
(Actions)

(5) Critical to Process, (2) Needed, ( ) No Relationship

External Customers

External Customer:
The user of an organization's
output who is not part
of an organization

Figure A-3

Internal Customer "A" Chart

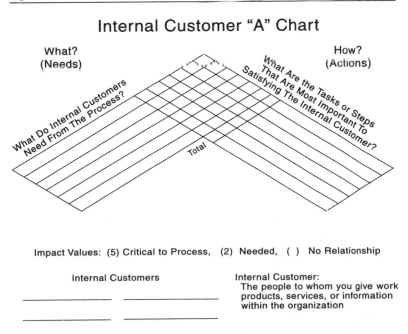

What?
(Needs)

How?
(Actions)

Impact Values: (5) Critical to Process, (2) Needed, ( ) No Relationship

Internal Customers

Internal Customer:
The people to whom you give work
products, services, or information
within the organization

Figure A-4

Process "A" Chart

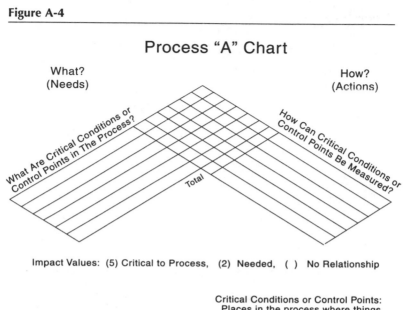

What? (Needs)   How? (Actions)

Impact Values: (5) Critical to Process, (2) Needed, ( ) No Relationship

Critical Conditions or Control Points:
Places in the process where things
could go wrong, causing complaints
or rework, places where measurements
should be considered

Figure A-5

Supplier "A" Chart

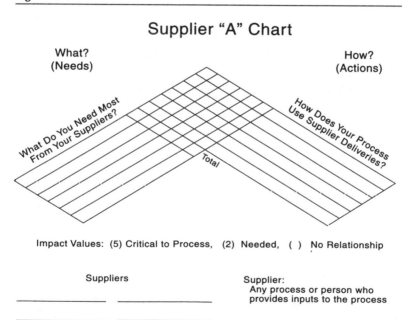

What? (Needs)   How? (Actions)

Impact Values: (5) Critical to Process, (2) Needed, ( ) No Relationship

Suppliers

Supplier:
Any process or person who
provides inputs to the process

_____ _____

_____ _____

Figure A-6

Process Mastering
Key Step Worksheet

Process:_____   Date: _____

Team Name:_____   Date to be Rechecked: _____

Key Step #	Key Step Name (Starts With a Verb)	Best Known Way	Tricks of The Trade	Consequences of Doing It Wrong
Handling Exceptions				
Process Measurements	What Is Measured	How It Is Measured	Target	Range

Figure A-7

Process Exception Report

Process Name:_____   **Process Master Date:** _____

Step Number	Reason For Change	Action Taken	Result	Initials	Date

Operator Comments: _____

_____

_____

Supervisor Response: Date: _____

1. No Action Taken.
   Why: _____

2. Process Master Review Required.

3. Problem Corrected.
   How: _____

Supervisor's Signature _____

Figure A-8

Process Master Sign-Off Sheet

Process Master Number: _____

Process Name: _____

Date: _____

Our process master team has identified and written down the best known ways to carry out our process. By signing below, I agree to follow the attached process master whenever possible. I understand that exceptional situations may force a temporary change in the process. When this happens, I will act in the best interests of my customers. I will also turn in a Process Master Exception Report of the temporary changes for possible updating of the process master.

Team Sponsor: _____

Team Leader: _____

Process Team Members:

_____   _____

_____   _____

_____   _____

_____   _____

Dates of Revisions: _____

                           _____

                           _____

                           _____

                           _____

Appendix B

PROCESS MASTERING CHECKLISTS

Process Master Meeting Checklist

Below is a list of questions that should be considered in evaluating the process of developing a process master. By answering these questions, the team has an opportunity to improve the process before beginning another process master. It may be helpful to share the results with other teams and team leaders.

1. Did the team follow the norms established at the start of the team meetings?

2. Have all team members helped to develop the Process Master?

3. Were the Customer Needs developed with external and internal customer input?

4. Do the Critical Conditions and Control Points cover realistic, measurable conditions in the process?

5. Were suppliers involved or considered in discussion of needs from suppliers?

6. Are needs statements clear, definable, and to the point? Do they avoid words such as: when needed, often, on time, soft, adequate, etc.?

7. Do flow chart steps begin with an action verb?

8. Have all Key Steps been identified especially all safety and environmental hazards?

9. Did the team use photos or drawings whenever appropriate?

10. Has the Process Master been put into a complete document for ready reference?

11. Have all employees involved with the process signed off that they agree to follow the Process Master?

12. Has a list of "parking lot" ideas been generated, and is there a plan to begin exploring their potential?

13. Has one or more important measurement been identified to monitor the health of this process? Have all the details such as who, what, when, where, and how the measurement(s) will be taken been worked out?

Team Chartering Checklist

Describe the process

List the people who work within the process:

What is the name of the process, and why was it chosen?

_____

What are the boundaries of the process (starting and ending points)? _____

List the people who work within the process:

_____

Who is the team leader/process owner?_____

Team composition

How many people do we want on the team?_____

Do we need an outside expert to brief the team or to be a part of the team?_____

Should suppliers or customers be a part of the team?_____

How will each shift be represented? _____

Logistics

What day and time will the team meet?_____

Have the team members been trained in process mastering?

_____

Are resources (meeting space, supplies, and clerical support) available? _____

What is the target date for sponsor review?_____

Cautions

What circumstances or work products, if any, would cause the sponsor to reject the work of the team?_____

_____

Will there be an adverse effect on surrounding processes or customers if this process is standardized? _____

Special needs

Does the sponsor expect any particular measurement(s) to be included in the process? _____

Trial Period Checklist

Following the period when the process master has been tried in the workplace, it is very important to review how it went. Below is a checklist to begin the evaluation.

1. Did everyone get trained in the best known way as described in the process master?

2. Did everyone understand the urgency and seriousness of following the process master?

3. Was the trial period long enough for everyone to try the process several times?

4. Did a person who is relatively unfamiliar with the process try to follow the process master?

5. Does the newly mastered process actually describe the way the work is done?

6. Are any steps over standardized? (No standardization needed?) Do any of the best known way descriptions have to be changed based on actual experience?

7. Do all the people who work in the process feel like co-owners, and do they know they are expected to be constantly searching for ideas that will allow the process to be improved?

8. Were any exceptions discovered?

9. Was the process master posted or made available to everyone?

10. Was the process owner identified, and was that responsibility accepted?

11. What data was generated? Are the process measurements that were chosen acceptable?

Appendix C

MEASURES

Accuracy of forecasts

Data entry errors

Actual time compared to estimate

Cost of customer complaints, by type

Actual variance from plan in dollars, time or %

Number of payments posted incorrectly

Number of incorrect new account documents

Number of days over branch cash limit

Days payable

Days receivable

Loans below minimum credit standards

Loans 30 days past due

Amounts of loans 30 days past due

Number/value of charged-off loans

Number of payments backlogged

Percent of applications not responded to in _____ days

Net charge-off dollars

Number of errors in funds transfers, by type

Number of tax returns not completed on time

Number of accounts overdrawn

Number of reports delivered late

CUSTOMER SERVICE

Customer orders for wrong product

Claims satisfaction

Variance from customer expectation or specification

Type and number of customer complaints

Gained and lost customer ratios

Complaints from downstream processes

Percent transaction errors

Completed credit applications

Number of payments processed

Average customer wait time

Number of checks not collected

Dollar amount of checks not collected

Number of calls not returned within _____ days

Number of participants served

ENGINEERING/RESEARCH & DEVELOPMENT

Response time

Number of new products developed

Value of new products developed

Number of process improvements

Dollar value of process improvements

Estimated contribution to profit/dollar of R&D costs

Number of drawing changes, by type

Number of projects more than _____ days old

HUMAN RESOURCES

Cost per hire

Number of suggestions submitted

Number of employees in training

Time to obtain replacement

Orientation cost per employee

Turnover rates, hourly and salaried

Number of grievances

Number of accidents

Percent absenteeism

Number of training hours

Time between accidents

Recruiting costs per recruit retained

Benefit costs per employee

Training costs per average number of employees

Percent new employees completing orientation within _____ days of hire

Worker's compensation costs per average number of employees

Percent correct answers on company knowledge tests

Number of fringe benefit complaints

Number of tardies/total employees

MANAGEMENT INFORMATION SYSTEMS

Minutes system is down/month

Programmers per dollar of sales

Programming backlog, in days

User entry-response time, seconds

Desktop equipment downtime, minutes/month

Number of users/computer technician

Service backlog, by type

Preventive maintenance hours, by type

Program maintenance hours

Number of reports delivered on time

Number of reports actually used

MAINTENANCE

Percent of time doing preventive maintenance

Cycle time from request until completion

Percent of jobs completed on time

Air flow, cubic feet per minute

Trouble calls per day

MARKETING

Number of customer surveys sent, by type
Percentage of customer surveys returned
Cold calls per day, by type
Calls on lost customers
Calls on competitors' customers

MATERIALS MANAGEMENT

Scrap rate, by type
Value of inventory/dollar of sales
Percent shrink
Pounds (kilos) of waste
Value of waste and scrap
Variance from inventory targets

PRODUCTION

Fill weights
Amount of overfill/container
Leaking containers
Seam thickness, mils
Seam strength, integrity
Overtime hours
Volume
Percent overtime hours

PRODUCTION SCHEDULING

Percent overtime attributed to scheduling
Percent on-time issuance of daily status reports
Percent of time operation starts _____ minutes past
    scheduled time

PURCHASING

Cost per anything
Delivery times

Percent orders received on time

Percent orders where price varies from original requisition

Percent shortages

Time from purchase order to receipt

Time lost waiting on materials

Number of internal product complaints per vendor

Dollar purchases, by type

Percent purchases/total sales

Purchasing costs/dollar amount of purchases

Processing time/number of requisitions

QUALITY

Defects per part

Dimensions of parts

Temperatures, heat and cool

Pressures, hydraulic and reactor

Percent fiber

Broken pallets per truckload

Defective cartons per load

Oil viscosity

Percent purity of materials

Processing time or temperature

Fill weights

Number of customer complaints, by type

Percent of quality checks completed

SALES

Gained/lost customer ratio

Calls per day

Costs per call

Value of gained business/lost business

Number of competitor's customers interviewed

Time to return calls

Number of customers/sales person

Customers, by type
Sales, by customer category
Sales increase, by customer type

SHIPPING

Loading/unloading time
Delivery times
Wrong shipments
Percent of orders shipped most economical way
Percent on-time shipments
Number of rejected shipments
Value (costs) of rejected shipments

STRATEGIC PLANNING

Percent utilization of manufacturing facilities
Number of employees involved in long-range planning
  activities
Contributions to key success factors

SUPPORT

Number of items misfiled/missing
Percent returned mail

TIMELINESS

Time to repair
Number of rings before phone is answered
Time between repairs
Percent down time, by machine
Down time
Elapsed time for processing insurance claims
Order backlog
Conveyor speed, revolutions per minute
Holes drilled between sharpening bits
Turnaround time, from order entry until delivery

Wasted Time and Materials

Number of spills
Number of leaks
Dollar cost of rework
Delays, by type
Number of delays, by type

Not-for-Profit Organizational Health Indices

The second list of outcomes was included for not-for-profit organizations, such as community-service agencies.

Comprehensive Child Care

Children exhibit age-appropriate physical skills
Children are school-ready for kindergarten

General Equivalency Degree Preparation

Participants obtain their GED certificates within one year
Participants are employed within six months of entering program

Outpatient Treatment for Substance Abusers

Adolescents increase knowledge about substance addiction
Adolescents change attitude toward substance abuse
Graduates remain drug-free six months after completion of program

Emergency Shelter Beds on Winter Nights

Number of homeless persons using the shelter

Volunteer Tutoring After School

Youths complete homework assignments
Youths perform at or above their grade level

FULL-DAY CHILD CARE FOR HOMELESS PRESCHOOLERS

Children engage in age-appropriate play
Children exhibit fewer symptoms of stress-related
regression

OVERNIGHT CAMPING FOR INNER-CITY BOYS

Boys learn outdoor survival skills
Boys develop and maintain positive peer relationships

COMMUNITY MEALS FOR SENIOR CITIZENS

Elderly patients are not homebound
Participants have social interaction with their peers
Participants eat a nutritious and varied diet
Seniors experience a decrease in social and health
problems

INTERPRETER SERVICES FOR NON-ENGLISH-SPEAKING PATIENTS

Patients access needed health care
Patients understand medical diagnosis
Patients use preventive measures and treatments
Patients show reduction in preventable illnesses

PERSONAL SAFETY TRAINING FOR RESIDENTS OF SUBSIDIZED APARTMENTS

Residents initiate neighborhood watch program
Residents plan and carry out building-security program
Personal and property attacks decline.

INDEX